GW00493007

# STRAY DOGS AND DARK HORSES

Selected Essays

on

Irish Writing and Criticism

─────────

Gerald Dawe

Abbey Press

First published in April 2000 in an edition of 1,000 copies,
250 of which are signed and numbered by the author

Abbey Press gratefully acknowledges the support of
The Arts Council of Northern Ireland

Abbey Press
*Newry Office*
Courtenay Hill, Newry, County Down
Northern Ireland, BT34 2ED

A CIP record for this book is available from the British Library

ISBN: 1 901617 20 3
Author: Dawe, Gerald
Title: Stray Dogs and Dark Horses
Format: 138 mm x 214 mm
2000

Design: Adrian Rice and David Anderson
Cover image: *Black Molly Long Legs* by Ross Wilson
Typesetting by David Anderson in 11/13pt Sabon
Printed by Nicholson & Bass Ltd, Belfast

*for
my mother*

# Acknowledgements

The author would like to acknowledge the following journals where most of the work contained in this book was originally published in somewhat different form: *Cambridge Review*, *Canadian Journal of Irish Studies*, *Crane Bag*, *Eire/Ireland*, *Fortnight*, *Graph*, *Honest Ulsterman*, *Irish Literary Supplement*, *Irish Review*, *The Irish Times*, Lagan Press, *Linen Hall Review*, *London Magazine*, *Poetry Ireland Review*, *Rhinoceros*, *Theatre Ireland* and *Threshold*.

Portions of the book were also delivered as lectures to The New Ireland Group, The John Hewitt Summer School, University of Aberdeen Conference on Region and Nation, The William Carleton Summer School, The Irish Writers Centre, Cúirt International Poetry Festival, The Badly-Loved Poetry Conference and also broadcast on R.T.E. Radio.

A special acknowledgement is kindly made to Louise Kidney for her help in getting together this material.

# About the Author

Gerald Dawe was born in Belfast in 1952. He moved to the west of Ireland in 1974. His books of poetry include *Sheltering Places*, *The Lundys Letter*, *Sunday School*, *Heart of Hearts* and *The Morning Train*. He has also published *Against Piety*, a collection of essays, and *The Rest is History*, a book about Belfast. He lives in Dún Laoghaire and teaches at Trinity College Dublin.

The Abbey Press also publish *The Rest is History* by Gerald Dawe.

# CONTENTS

I still have my imagination and in its impregnable innocence it will keep me going until the end of my days. All this compulsion to 'understand' everything fills me with horror. I love the unexpected.

Louis Buñuel, *My Last Sigh*

# TIOCFAIDH ÁR LÁ

When Mrs. Thatcher, the then prime minister of Great Britain and Northern Ireland, met two Irish clerics, Cardinal Ó Fiaich and Bishop James Lennon on 1 July 1981 at Downing Street, she was, according to David Beresford,

> ... waiting for them at the top of the stairs, on the first-floor landing, and gushed a welcome ... They started with the usual pleasantries, but quickly moved onto the prison issue.

'Will someone please tell me why they are on hunger strike?' asked the Prime Minister. 'I have asked so many people. Is it to prove their virility?'

Two months earlier, Francis Hughes had died on hunger strike, and in the month of August Tom McIlwee was also to die. Hughes and McIlwee were cousins, in their mid-twenties, born within a year of each other (1956–57), from Bellaghy, County Derry. They were buried together, 'in a new section of the cemetery at St. Mary's Church':

> Their tombstone is inscribed in Irish which Tom – battling to learn the language even as he was dying – would have particularly appreciated. And Frank would have liked the wording: 'Among the warriors of the Gael may his soul rest'.

David Beresford's *Ten Men Dead* is full of such chilling contrasts. How is it possible, one asks, for two islands so physically, economically, culturally and socially close as Britain and Ireland, to be so grotesquely divided. History and language?

In his collection of essays, *Less Than One*, Joseph Brodsky often returns to the inextricable meshing of expression and experience. Discussing Andrei Platonov, he sees the Russian novelist as 'a millenarian writer if only because he attacks the very carrier of millenarian sensibility in Russian society: the language itself – or, to put it in a more graspable fashion, the revolutionary eschatology embedded in the language'. Brodsky goes on to define the roots of Russian millenarianism in the following terms:

> On the mental horizon of every millenarian movement there is always a version of a New Jerusalem, the proximity to which is determined by the intensity of sentiment. The idea of God's city being within reach is in direct proportion to the religious fervour in which the entire journey originates. The variations on this theme include also a change of the entire world order, and a vague, but all the more appealing because of that, notion of a new time, in terms of both chronology and quality. (Naturally, transgressions committed in the name of getting to a New Jerusalem fast are justified by the beauty of the destination.) When such a movement succeeds, it results in a new creed. If it fails, then, with the passage of time and the spread of literacy, it degenerates into utopias, to peter out completely in the dry sands of political science and the pages of science fiction. However, there are several things that may somewhat rekindle soot-covered embers. It's either severe oppression of the population, a real, most likely military peril, a sweeping epidemic, or some substantial chronological event, like the end of a millennium or the beginning of a new century.

Somewhat later in the same essay, 'Catastrophes in the Air', Brodsky remarks that the 'first casualty of any discourse about utopia – desired or already attained – is grammar; for language, unable to keep with this line of thought, begins to gasp in the subjunctive mood and starts to gravitate toward categories and constructions of a rather timeless denomination. As a consequence of this, the ground starts to slip out from under even the simplest nouns, and they gradually get enveloped in an aura of arbitrariness.' Platonov, according to Brodsky, 'was able to reveal a self-destructive eschatological element within the language itself, and that, in turn, was of extremely revealing consequences to the revolutionary eschatology with which history supplied him as the subject matter'.

The image of Platonov which Brodsky presents, in contrast to Kafka, Joyce or Beckett 'who narrate quite natural tragedies of their alter egos', itself verges on the apocalyptic:

Platonov speaks of a nation which in a sense has become the victim of its own language ... he tells a story about this very language, which turns out to be capable of generating a fictitious world, and then falls into grammatical dependence on it.

The ten Republican paramilitaries who died on hunger-strike were mostly from old country families. Three were Belfast men and one from Derry city. The oldest of them was born in 1951 and the youngest in 1957. With remission, nine of the ten would have been out of Long Kesh in 1987. *Ten Men Dead* moves with close and careful reconstruction through the awful months when the prisoners inside the Kesh fought off attempts at 'criminalisation'. 'Instead of pulling out, Britain dug in even deeper, reimposing direct rule after a brief experiment in power-sharing and devising the three-prong strategy: Ulsterisation, normalisation and criminalisation – which found one form of physical expression in the building of the H-Blocks.' The criminalisation policy, according to Beresford, sought to deny

... a belief held dear by Republican Ireland – that husbands, wives, boyfriends, girlfriends, parents, grandparents and great-grandparents who had suffered and died for Irish independence had done so in the high cause of patriotism.

As Terence MacSwiney, Lord Mayor of Cork, had put it in his inaugural speech (1920);

... the contest on our side is not one of rivalry or vengeance, but of endurance. It is not those who can inflict the most, but those that can suffer the most who will conquer.

And, in an essay, MacSwiney hailed: 'the day when the consciousness of the country will be electrified with a great deed or a great sacrifice and the multitude will break from lethargy or prejudice and march with a shout for freedom in a true, a brave and a beautiful sense.'

First by refusing to wear uniforms, then through the 'blanket' protest, the 'no wash' and the 'dirty' protests, the prisoners were finally cornered, through failure to achieve their basic objectives ('the five demands') which were for recognition of their political status. Rather than ending the blanket protest, abandoning the hunger strike and organising themselves very much as the British had done in POW camps during World War II, the Republican prisoners were, as Beresford states, drawn back to MacSwiney and those who endure the most. 'It was not a practical approach [one of the prisoners maintained] ... you came out of it with moral superiority, but the Movement already has that ... and so did not need to do it. What the prisoners had to do was win the battle and in order to do that they needed to be more flexible, to adopt a two-pronged approach – try to destroy the system by working within it while at the same time standing outside it.'

The harking back to previous generations and times so totally different from the present gives a kind of hallucinatory quality to the story. The isolation of the Provo leadership 'living in something of a political cocoon' is compounded by the innocence of the hunger-strikers. Hardened by injustice, risk, guilt and insularity, their expectations of life were heavily guarded from childhood by sentinels of nationalist piety. The religious force which Fr. Faul refers to when blaming churchmen 'in a way for what happened: saying that, after all, they taught people to imitate Christ, so the Church can hardly complain when they go out and do just that' blends with the established, traditionalist cultural imperatives of the Irish language and the GAA to reinforce the utopianism instilled in the Catholic youth of Northern Ireland. When this confronts a force, state or system totally hostile to such things, the only recourse seems to be through the logic of utopianism itself. The future (a United Ireland) matters more than the present (a divided province). So one gives oneself literally to posterity – '... those that can suffer most ... will conquer'. The grammatical dependence is already there; the prejudice, bigotry and oppression hang like a cloud constantly in the background. A new 'pure' world can be generated in its place:

> Hunger-striking, when taken to the death, has a sublime quality about it; in conjunction with terrorism it offers a consummation of murder and self-sacrifice which in a sense can legitimise the violence which precedes and follows it. If after killing or sharing in a

conspiracy to kill – for a cause one shows oneself willing to die for the same cause, a value is adduced which is higher than that of life itself. But the obverse is also true: failure to die can discredit the cause. To scream for mercy at the foot of the gallows – or nod at the saline drip as kidneys and eyes collapse and the doctor warns of irreversible damage – is to affirm that there is no higher value than life and none worthy of condemnation than those who take it.

Inevitably, David Beresford's book makes one ask: what did these young men die for? But no answer presents itself. Instead, Beresford's strict grasp of narrative falters in the concluding pages and blurs into a self-enfolding, fatalistic assumption that Irish history is duty-bound to repeat itself ad infinitum. The hunger-strikers 'died for a cause far more ancient than the grey walls of Long Kesh prison'. But people do not die on hunger strike for a cause because it is old. Perplexed by the precise reasons and the political significance of whatever they may be, Beresford inserts clichés: 'the age-old struggle', 'time immemorial', the 'centuries-old struggle' – all subsumed in the stretched theatrical context of W.B. Yeats' play *The King's Threshold*:

> When I and these are dead
> We should be carried to some windy hill
> To lie there with uncovered face awhile
> That mankind and that leper there may know
> Dead faces laugh. King! King! Dead faces laugh.

But the point of *The King's Threshold* is lost: Seanchan, the poet, stands up for poetry, the imagination, and refuses to become a mere crony of King Guaire and his council-chamber.

At times, *Ten Men Dead* reads like the literature the prisoners were themselves reading: Kipling, Wilde and Eilís Dillon. Bobby Sands makes a special request:

> I was wondering … that out of the goodness of all yer hearts you could get me one miserly book and try to leave it in: the Poems of Ethna Carberry-*cissy*. That's really all I want, last request as they say. Some ask for cigarettes, others for blindfolds, yer man asks for poetry.

In some way that I have not been able to define, the lives of these ten men were surrounded by a kind of estranged ether, an emotional and intellectual current no longer earthed to the core realities of Ireland as it is today. Unquestionably, they knew and had unforgettable first-hand experience of sectarianism and militarism. Equally, the cultural idealism which has emerged out of this situation has brought with it a sense of dignity long denied by the political state of Northern Ireland. It is, though, the complex contradiction which manifests itself through their double-life, as bombers and murderers and as freedom-fighters and Irish soldiers, which defeats me. It seems fuelled by the early tragic world of Irish peasants which was converted into the poetic stock of Yeats' revivalist prose and ballads of the late nineteenth century. It defies any bearing to the social and cultural reality of the country as a whole, and even less to the deprivation of Belfast. Rhetoric is a pitiless word when lives are laid on the line:

> We re-confirm and pledge 'our' full confidence and support to you and march on with you to the Irish Socialist Republic.

If the *Ten Men Dead* were victims of language, then it is because of a myth that nationalism sows in the heart. Achievements in the Republic – of a welfare system, an adequate education, jobs and houses for all; social freedom and cultural independence; confidence and outwardness – are historically vulnerable. Militant nostalgia is no challenge in this context. As Salman Rushdie remarked, it is to discover 'that one's entire picture of the world is false, and not only false but based upon a monstrosity. What a task for any individual: the reconstruction of reality from rubble.' In a way, the dominant forces of nationalism have brought little to the ordinary people but the sweet breathless banality of 'Is it to prove their virility?' or the shattered wrecks of men, 'prison-pale skin stretched across paradoxically young skull-like faces with what Bobby Sands had once described as "that awful stare, of the pierced, or glazed eyes." '

[1987]

# WITH BEASTS AND DEVILS

*Calling someone a monster does not make him more guilty; it makes him less so by classing him with beasts and devils.*

– MARY McCARTHY

*The Shankill Butchers* by Martin Dillon is a harrowing book. It deals with a ghastly period in the sickly underworld of Belfast's sectarian life, and anyone who lived through that time in the 1970s, who knows the geography of these outrages and the people who were tortured and did the torturing, will naturally want to forget. The newspaper reports of the trials of these men – who methodically and determinedly brutalised, dehumanised and slaughtered their way through the mid '70s, leaving in their wake some thirty working-class Catholics and Protestants dead – make for terrifyingly grim reading. But why, one has to ask, has this Belfast world of violence, pathological hatred, squalid introversion and appalling narrow-mindedness not been exposed before? How can the miserable lives of bigots seek the darkness of anonymity and get away with it?

I was reminded of these questions constantly when reading Martin Dillon's brave book. It must have been a heart-rending job to absorb into himself the disgraceful acts of the Shankill butchers and the arbitrariness with which their victims were picked. All that mattered was 'to get a Taig'. But that act alone was earthed, as Dillon so rightly says, to an environment 'fuelled by extreme prejudice ... developed since childhood and which found an outlet in acts so violent that they could only have been committed by a psychopath'. In linking the psychopathology of these murderers to the prejudice of northern Irish society and, in particular, of Belfast, Martin Dillon has established a shatteringly simple truth about that society. Namely, the cost to it of being a self-divided society, based upon intolerance and ignorance; a condition which may lead eventually towards disintegration and collapse, if not of 'the State' – which looks remarkably resilient – then of 'the People'.

Ironically this condition has very little to do with politics since there is very little real political discussion in the North. What clusters around the religious distinction between Protestant and Catholic cultures is a desperate longing for identity in a society that lacks a common one, civically established and accepted by the majority of people who actually live there.

When the Provos destroyed Belfast with their civilian-targeted bombs, and the UVF and UDA assassinated Catholics and their own 'traitors', the corruption of Belfast's sectarian past spilled on to the streets again. As Dillon says:

> Northern Ireland has a society where prejudice is so deeply rooted that extermination rather than derision is the likely outcome when nothing is done to erode it. In most instances the victims of prejudice are not the combatants but the innocent. It is difficult, of course, to eradicate prejudice but serious and concerted attempts should have been made to replace it with tolerance and more positive attitudes within the churches and the educational system.

These minimal recommendations were studiously avoided in the 1950s and '60s. By the end of that decade it was too late. The jails are now packed with the perpetrators of some of the worst murders ever done by young men to their fellow citizens in these islands. As Dillon points out, the Shankill Butchers were mass murderers but given the extent of prejudice 'which is endemic in Northern Ireland there was an inevitability that it would end up in "extermination".'

This is precisely what the 1970s and '80s in Northern Ireland became: a moral and psychic landscape traversed by men and women dedicated to violence. There are no ifs and buts about this fact, yet, for some reason, we try to sidestep this basic truth. Where are the books about violence and recent history; sectarianism; the struggle against both; the make-up and reality of paramilitary life?

We live in a society which has methodically refused, institutionally, culturally and politically, to own up to lassitude and acceptance of violence as a means of effecting change. Dillon casts light on the last two decades of life in the North and the way this experience is channelled through ideals and assumptions rarely in touch with human reality.

'While I was in [Long Kesh] Gerry Adams advocated the use of explosives as a means of stepping up the IRA campaign. I interpreted that to mean car bombs which later wrecked Belfast and caused untold casualties in 1972 and 1973', one informant is quoted as saying in Dillon's book, putting in context the backdrop to what was unleashed by the Shankill Butchers a little later. As Dillon says in his conclusion, 'Terrorists are impervious to expressions of morality even when such expressions are part of a public disavowal of violence.' His hope is that his book will 'at least have created the basis for debate about the nature of prejudice.'

The paramilitaries who populate Dillon's book and the real world outside their existence are fed by, and in turn feed, the hunger of a people whose lives are distorted in a twisted society. The transcendence of that world takes the form of dominating it through violence, brash displays of power; acting, as Belfast jargon has it, 'the big man'. When this act turns into the phantasmagoria of literal control over the life and death of an individual, a street, a district, the carved-up compass of a society, anything can happen. In such delusions the human form, like the victims cut and tortured by the Shankill Butchers or the incinerated remains of the La Mon bombing, is despised as weak and flawed. Mistakes become tactical errors. The individual literally gets in the way. There are, simply, no problems, except logistical ones. People, in a perverse logic, do not count.

Martin Dillon's book illustrates the grim reality of such fantasy. For the Butchers, most of whom are still behind bars, their world really was, on this telling, a despicable place. Their dependencies were real enough: drink, violence as a way of life, each other; cocooned from outsiders who might prey upon them and in some way show them up – the peculiarly northern fear of being, not captured, but 'found out'. This fear breaks through, finally, as they are apprehended and in custody: under the light of day, their defences crumble. Reality breaks through; there is no ideological or mental barrier between the means and ends of what was done. One of them, who had been involved in particularly gruesome throat-cuttings broke down, cried and said: 'My head's away with it'. He also asked himself if he was 'wise'.

Another of the gang, after sentencing, ended up in prison close by the Provisional IRA leader, Brendan Hughes, who remarked of the UVF man: 'He talked a lot to me and was intrigued to know about republicanism. I felt that suddenly here was a guy who had been involved in killing a lot of people and who had probably mouthed political slogans but never understood them ... The one thing which struck me about [the man] was his need to have even someone like me as a friend. He demonstrated a curious loyalty to me ...'

Whatever the presumption of moral supremacy here ('a guy who had been involved in killing a lot of people' and 'probably mouthed political slogans but never understood them' is how a lot of people would see IRA activists) the dependency and tension revealed in these extracts bear directly upon the appalling contrast between the dreamlike, insulated state and 'outside' reality of the paramilitary world. Between these extremes, like an obsessive metronome, the activist is eventually drawn back and forth, with increasingly narrow odds on his or her personal survival but also a decreasing likelihood of their seeing actual political change as a direct result of their actions.

This might well be the lesson of *The Shankill Butchers*: that violence does not make anything change for real. The victim is buried alongside the torturer; the bomber with the bombed. The terrible misreading of political possibility which took place in the North during the 1970s and '80s inside the various factions only led to a further twist in the spiral of self-defeating violence and now, twenty odd years down the road, one has to ask: what has really changed and what will be the difference when we reach the twenty-fifth anniversary of 'the troubles'?

What *The Shankill Butchers* also proves is that lacking a true sense of political and cultural well-being, split against itself, denied any wider vision from either school or church, the North has, in reality, teetered from one subdued crisis to another. Those who ruled it, either before or since partition, had very little interest in what went on in the little and not-so-little streets and avenues of Belfast. The police were left to mop up after the latest atrocity.

Martin Dillon's *The Shankill Butchers* is fearsome. It will not be palatable to those commentators in the English and US press who like their historical cake to be neat and uncomplicated by vile reality. The book will also pierce the banal coverage by much of the Republic's media, bored and bothered as they are by 'Europe' and the soft-centred nationalism of their own gradually disappearing past.

I can only think of those streets where I grew up and walked with girlfriends, going home after dances in town, or parties, without a care in the world, and realise how that time will never come back to those who were so cruelly torn from this life by men and women who lived just a few streets away. It will take a huge leap of imagination before this dammed-up tragedy is released and understood and overcome by all those who physically and morally want to reconstitute the meaning of home. Hundreds of thousands have done this daily in the North, a common victory taken far too much for granted on the island of Ireland as a whole.

[1990]

# ANECDOTES OVER A JAR

*The lesson of our time is that Irish writers cannot any longer go on writing about Ireland, or for Ireland within the narrow confines of the traditional Irish life concept; it is too slack, too evasive, too intense.*

– Sean O'Faoláin

I was in Holland in 1981 with Richard Murphy, on a reading tour, and in Amsterdam we were separately interviewed. The keen radio interviewer wanted me to talk about 'violence' and 'political repression' and later on, in a taxi, I heard my own voice, with estranged gravitas, struggling to answer him. It was obvious that the good Dutch radio man had clear ideas about Ireland and wanted to have them confirmed in double-quick time before moving on to the next item – William Burroughs, if I am not mistaken, who was sitting in a marble-like pool of silence, cane-in-hand and in Trilby hat.

It was my first experience of the weight of assumption and expectation which bears upon the two words 'Irish Poet'. Five years later, in a packed hotel in Sydney, for the city's Poetry Festival, the sign on the door revealed 'Irish Poet' reading along with Les Murray and Tom Murphy. Through the steamy night, lots of people milled in and out but, half-way through my stint, a (drunken) voice came from the back of the hall: 'You're not following in the footsteps of Heaney'. This question, complaint or statement (I wasn't sure which) was patently true since I stood reading my own poems. But I understood and sympathised with what the man meant.

Probably an expatriate, here he was amongst a mixed bunch of 'ex-pats' of all kinds and on stage was this poet, from Ireland mark you, reading poems not about the Ireland he knew, or thought he knew: O'Faoláin's 'traditional life-concept'. And, if you weren't insulted, the poet was actually talking about Edward Carson, for Christ's sake, and little towns in the North no one ever heard of. What he was hearing simply did not fit and he was having none of it.

Another quirky illustration might be sufficient to indicate the weight of expectation that lies upon this notion of the Irish poet, whether at home or abroad. It is a fascinating subject in itself since its powerful influence, particularly via the States, has rarely been touched upon by critics of writing from Ireland.

I met an EC literary journalist accompanied by an avid Irish intellectual trend-spotter. In the brief exchange, I was asked for an opinion on several questions: about 'the loss of Irish', colonial history, identity crises, and the role of women writers in modern Ireland. This menu of issues, of which I had personally little experience, amounted to an agenda and it became crystal-clear that poetry had very little to do with it, except to serve as a springboard for someone else's flight of fancy. Irish poets were influenced by Irish poets and Irish history, O.K. Game, set and match. As for Europe …?

When I muttered something about coming from a Protestant background in Belfast and living in the west of Ireland, a professional smile glazed over what remained of their time. Critical comment on that background, indeed, on any sense of alternative influences, arguments or literary ideals, went out the window.

◆

Three random experiences. But behind them there are other conversations and impressions which illustrate the kind of busy and processed responses poets in Ireland must resist in their work if they are to remain truly themselves as artists. There is, and probably always has been, a shifting agenda of themes and issues which 'Irish' literature is seen as addressing. In the 1970s, for instance, it was 'The North'; in the 1980s it was 'Women' and 'Regionalist Writing', and speculatively, the

1990s could well see the received wisdom switch back to 'The South' again.

These crude generalisations are nevertheless influential both in a popular sense and in strict terms of criticism (i.e. what gets written about) as they underpin certain kinds of public space and esteem (i.e. recognition) in which the individual poet lives and writes.

◆

The story goes that Ireland is coming down with poets. Certainly, it is much easier to have a poem or collection of poetry published in Ireland today than it was, say, twenty years ago. This is a 'good thing' but what it really means in artistic and critical terms is another matter. All too easily, the books go unheeded in the literary pages of the newspapers and the few literary journals cannot hope to keep pace. The undiscriminating media happily obliterate the work of art in a haze of well-meaning publicity surrounding this writer or that and their ability to make themselves and/or their writing 'accessible', 'controversial' and so forth. Where is the artistic daring, one asks, as the poem evaporates? Literary standards are equated with elitism or derided as academic when really it is 'period styles' that should be criticised – outdated or hackneyed themes; stale language; flat rhetoric; predictable feelings. Could there be, for instance, an equivalent version of Alfred Alvarez's *The New Poetry*, the publication of which in the mid-1960s (with the brilliant Jackson Pollock *Convergence* as cover) challenged so many imaginations and critical sensibilities, both old and new? Or of Donald Hall's updated version of Michael Roberts' *Faber Book of Modern Verse* whose presence on 'A' level courses throughout Northern Ireland and Britain during the late 1960s enlightened an entire generation of poets and readers in a handful of years, along with the marvellous BBC Radio school programmes on poetry, accompanied by their extraordinary texts?

The late 1970s and 1980s really mark an epoch in which poets and poetry became sexy, an acceptable career move with its own structure of blandishments, self-promotion and sales-pitch at a time, ironically, of economic recession, political meanness and cultural bonanza.

But to go back to that term 'academic'. As someone who flits between two worlds – of trying to live as a writer and also help keep a roof over my family's heads through teaching – the extent to which the life of the intelligence is belittled in Ireland, often in a misconstrued support for the priority of the imagination, never fails to surprise me. Indeed ignorance of the poetic traditions of writing is sometimes seen as a guarantee and index of artistic integrity. This perverse and deeply damaging notion is related to the persistent, bathetic belief in the poetic 'personality' as a hero.

The problem is the basic uncertainty about the value of contemporary literary work, whereas the public role and social occasion of its expression are more eagerly assimilated in the Irish literary culture. This avoids the awkward, time-consuming business of assessing, considering and vindicating artistic worth which becomes a matter of anecdotes over a jar.

As in our politics, personality is inflated with meaning and thence to the ghastly patronage of 'the character'. It is amazing, too, how many writers, including younger ones, seem to connive at this recognition. The main thrust of our generalisations about art, writing and the imagination (all such vague, abstract words in comparison with the homely 'saying' of a poem) reflect this unease. For in some deep-seated fashion poets in Ireland must not take their work seriously. This is where the myth of the 'Irish Poet' intercedes, bolstered very often by archaic ideas and misconceptions about the country as a whole. For example, Irish writers are not, generally speaking, badly done by; their work is published relatively easily; there are various venues, festivals, art centres, magazines, television and radio programmes interested in promoting and conferring reputations on people as poets. The Arts Councils do fork out bursaries and other monies. Aosdána pays people to concentrate upon their writing. UK and US reading circuits, publishers, universities and so on, are receptive to Irish poets. In other words, as poets we do not actually *suffer* directly from repression, political violence, the loss of our language ...

Yet for all that there is the sense of claustrophobia, of a kind of repressiveness embedded in the culture and internalised by those writers conscious of their 'privileged' position within Irish society and troubled by both sets of circumstances. Familiarity may well breed a contempt of sorts when there is not sufficient critical respect given to the art of poetry. And there is, too, the business of just how independent writers in Ireland can be, given the close ties between the writing establishment, the state and the commercial world.

Who is looking at the effects and influences of this liaison upon standards in the arts? Does it lead to conformity or artistic compromise with a view to what gets bought, read or produced? Who are the people in Ireland entrusted with promoting standards in the literary or visual arts? What do we know of them; what are their qualifications in fulfilling such creative, editorial or judgmental roles? Should we even care?

Great hatred, little room? Not quite – more like anxiety, that verges on neurosis, surrounding the social and political orthodoxies and conformism of a culture which is still in curious ways unsure of itself. It is a culture, moreover, which is contradictorily ambivalent about its need for recognition from other cultures, particularly English and American, and peculiarly conscious of having to live up to *their* expectations of what Irish culture is, along with the sort of things we are meant to write about it.

I think of Sean O'Faoláin again, of his isolation too, and his telling remark:

> It is a matter of bravely and clearsightedly accepting the tensions of one's own being, or relentlessly challenging the life about one with their sharpest questions, of looking, then, far and wide, in time and place, for others who have been in some like conflict ... saying to them, 'That was how it seemed to you! Here is how it strikes me,' and seize one's pen, for them and one's self.

[1990]

29

# A REAL LIFE ELSEWHERE
## Tom Murphy and Thomas Kilroy

Thomas Murphy's two plays *Bailegangaire* and *Conversations on a Homecoming* give to the provincial sense of place a status of lyrical reality – to use Joseph Brodsky's description of the poetry of Derek Walcott. There is a tremendous generosity in both plays, bestowing upon the characters the human grace of being, for good or ill, just what they are. In the reveries of Mommo in *Bailegangaire* or the coded barbs and nostalgias of the characters in *Conversations*, Murphy does not so much present insights into people, as let them ramble on. They are trapped by what they say or, like Mommo, imprison others in their story-telling. By her indomitable spirit, Mommo controls Mary and Dolly, her grand-daughters, as they come to terms with their own stories. Buried in her bed, sucking sweets or supping milk, Mommo spins out a yarn like a web, holding fast the strands of attachment, despoiled sexuality and festering guilt. Yeats' 'wasteful virtues' were never as earthy as these.

Often, too, what is not said is the killing thing, like the opening and closing of *Conversations*: the 17-year-old Anne 'stands motionless, staring blankly out of the window, her expression simple and grave', the epitome of a young gentle hope that life is worth living after all the mouthing, resentment and egotism which surrounds her in the White House pub in the 1970s in east Galway.

*Conversations* follows a customary path. The returned Yank, Michael Ridge, a failed actor, arranges to meet some old pals in the local pub. It had been their centre, under the tutelage of J. J., who had sought to inspire in them a spirit of defiant independence. The ideal, as the play progresses, is shown up as a false god. 'People like yourself – people like yourself – ready to believe, get excited, follow to death an old bollocks with a borrowed image, any old J. J. who had read a book on American politics or business methods. Jesus, images: fuckin' neon shadows', as the embittered Tom remarks.

In dealing with the loss of idealism and coping with the actual world, Michael is assisted by Junior, who cares more for the simple allurements of unattainable sex and the ease of drink than any other of the debated desires. The local bank-clerk, Josephine, while never present on the stage, is like a cardboard cut-out, gross in her sexual appeal: 'She's big. No bother there, sham.'

Sex is the tinder that so readily ignites the raw frustrations of the group, but the tension the returned Yank brings to them is an exaggerated sense of their own failures: having gone nowhere, having seemingly achieved nothing.

In the middle of this is Tom, the teacher and one-time writer ('Now! The great writer: Did ye read his great socialist piece in *Boys' Own*', taunts Junior), and his half-rejection of J. J. (who also does not appear on stage but whose presence is central to *Conversations*):

> Is, was, always will be. A slob. He's probably crying and slobbering on somebody's shoulder now this very minute, somewhere around Galway. Missus in there [J. J.'s wife] treats him as if he were a child.

The curious thing about Tom's attitude to J. J., and the idealism he had stood for, is that Tom is also dependent upon his mother and upon his sour, love-hate relationship with the 40-year-old Peggy, his fiancée of ten years' standing. '... Stop making a show of yourself,' he exclaims but is quite prepared, as the night and drink wears on, to expose himself:

> ... despite us, the representatives of the rising cultural minorities aforementioned, what is going on now, this minute in Paddy Joe Daly's? 'Put th' fuckin' blanket on the ground.' But Paddy Joe Daly is not the enemy. He may personify it, the bullets in his bandy legs may symbolise it, the antics of his lump of a wife may dramatise it. But no – No! – the real enemy – the big one! – that we shall overcome, is the country-and-western system itself. Unyielding, uncompromising, in its drive for total sentimentality. A sentimentality I say that would have us all an unholy herd of Sierra Sues, sad-eyed inquisitors, sentimental

Nazis, fascists, sectarianists, black-and-white-shirted nationalists, with spurs-a-jinglin', all ridin' down the trail to Oranmore. Aw great, I knew I'd make ye all happy.

The energy of the language is almost a dramatic compensation for the stasis which envelops Murphy's people. Words become alternatives to living – they are all that is left:

Tom:       ... I can't feel anything about anything anymore.
Michael:   I know.
Tom:       What?
Michael:   I know what you mean.
Tom:       You're the only friend I have ... Wha'?
Michael:   Mutual.
Tom:       Say something.
Michael:   (*Quietly*) ... Yahoo?
Tom:       Did J.J. admire me?
Michael:   Yeh.
Tom:       (*To himself*) But what good is that? I don't think he understood my (*sighs*) situation. Isn't that what people want? What? A bit of clarity and sanity. Definition. Facts. Wha'? ... Did he admire me?
Michael:   Yeh.

There are several simultaneous conversations going on in *Conversations*. As the characters tell jokes and stories, they also use different kinds of language, 'put-on' voices such as Tom pretending to be Fr. Connolly (also known as Benny Diction) or Peggy singing deliberately off-key and 'poshly' distorting the words of the song she loves. This is a mark, too, of the embarrassment and reluctance to be taken seriously; the fear that taking their lives seriously would mean change, courage and risk – attributes which neither church nor state had fostered but had, instead, repressed or compromised.

Uncertainty masks their sense of themselves and the only sure thing is ownership of the familiar and habitual. When Michael sets up a meeting with J. J.'s daughter, Anne, Tom and Liam, drunk after the disorderly night, close in on him:

Liam:   Don't infringe.
Tom:    Liam's territory. Right, Liam.

In *Conversations*, there is a profound black despair which, infrequently, surfaces. Humour, bravado that verges on the slapstick (with Junior in particular) and caricature, like Liam ('the worst type of ponce of a modern fuckin' gombeen man') keep the wolf from the door even as the characters hunger for a real life elsewhere, in London or the States.

It is a terrible indictment of Irish life. What makes it so powerful is its vitality: the unforced containment of human extremity in Murphy's plays is reminiscent of Flannery O'Connor's stories. Both shun any form of patronising, authorial explanation. Like O'Connor, Murphy gives 'naturalism' a new meaning. Of the many playwrights writing in Ireland today, none has so sure a grasp of the community out of which they came, along with the ability to condemn that reality but not the people involved.

◆

The relation between 'knowing one's place' and leaving it, a kind of *Conversations* in reverse, is the subject of Thomas Kilroy's *Double Cross*.

Kilroy doubles back on the notion of the 'Emigrant's Return' by inspecting the performance of two Irishmen abroad – Brendan Bracken and William Joyce (Lord Haw-Haw). As Kilroy remarks in his 'Author's Note':

> This play attempts to deal with one kind of mobility, one kind of action across the barriers, the restrictive codes which separate countries from one another. It is the kind of action which is usually called treason.

What makes *Double Cross* so different from Murphy's plays is the play's expectations of the audience. It is a play which assumes the maturity of everyone – actor and audience, reader and critic – to accept highly conscious theatrical terms of reference.

Kilroy's characterisation, for instance, does not follow customary Irish theatrical practice. His characters are isolated figures, caught in a world of their own making, outside the support-systems of both community and the consoling rationale of being seen as 'rebels'. This confounds people who expect the either/or of role-playing – good/bad, hero/anti-hero – because Kilroy's characters inhabit the middle way.

He has previously selected 'characters' on the basis of this uniqueness: Mr. Roche in *The Death and Resurrection of Mr. Roche* and Matt Talbot in *Talbot's Box*, for example. They all assume an exemplary life, torn between solitude and involvement: at times victims, at other times almost victors. It is not so much their motivation which Kilroy explores as their fate, because his imagination tracks points of crisis rather than continuities. This involves his creating stage devices out of the ordinary: the imprisoning box of *Talbot's Box*, the video screen in *Double Cross* and the travelling theatre of *Madame MacAdam*. His language too has varied from the calm reserved English of the overseeing narrator in his [first] novel *The Big Chapel*, to the Blakean intensities of Talbot's Dublinese. *Double Cross* follows suit.

Kilroy writes for his characters a polished prose that only rage breaks through – in Lord Haw-Haw's final speech, for example, or in Bracken's collapse, fire-watching with the Warden from the roof of the Admiralty:

> (A sudden, heavy explosion, all lights out and a single cry. Bracken in a flickering light.) Bracken: (Deep fear) Daddy! Please – no! Mammy, Mammy! (At first faltering) My father, my father who is, my father was (Low, strong Tipperary accent). Me father was wan of the lads, so he was, wan of the hillside men. He took the oath. He was out in the tenants' war of eighty-nine. Bejasus, I was. I knew the treason prisoners of sixty-five. They were all great friends of yer father, so they were, the men that rotted away in Pentonville and Portland but bechrist their time will come again and when it does –
> Warden: (Voice out of the darkness) Mr. Bracken! Are you all right, sir?
> Bracken: (Irish accent)'Come here, Peter, me son. Come here a minnit, little man. You'll stand up for Ireland, won't you, boy, when you grow up, not like that brother of yours in the corner, Brendan-Brendy, the little scut, Mammy's pet, always whinging and bawling, four eyes – (English accent) Leave me alone! Leave me alone!

It is a lurid and deeply pathetic confession, fearful in being unexpected, so totally 'out of character' until Bracken regains his 'English' poise.

What drives *Double Cross* to its perverse conclusion is not a dramatic balancing of character, plot or, as with Murphy, the sheer effusion of language. Kilroy's theatre is a haunted place. There are fragments of faith and racial myth pulsing in the foreheads of the intense, comical, grotesque men as they try to play out their fantasies of an authentic life separated from the cramped demands of home and the idealised fatherland. Ultimately destroyed by this ever-elusive balance, Bracken and Joyce become Cain and Abel in pin-striped suits and garish uniforms: mock men succumbing to their own images of themselves.

What Kilroy achieves in *Double Cross* is to restore to Irish theatre the value of ideas and of how and why people do things because of what they believe should be admired or emulated. The classic colonised condition, in other words, is the yearning for acceptable standards.

Bracken's assimilation into British 'Society' was, like William Joyce's disgust at its confidence and conceit, a deeper sign of self-hate and showed itself in attitudes to the 'common' man:

> But I was about to say, my friends. There is no perfection without fire, no quickening without the burning lime, no redemption without ash. All you earnest believers in the perfectibility of man, attend! When the first great fire burned, the ice melted and the monkey stood upright in that incredible heat of the young sun. His brain expanded in its box. Words came from his mouth. Words refined the hanging jaw. And the nose melted into its human proportion. When the second great fire comes man will be burned out of his imperfection and into the shape of his dreams.

The deranged apocalyptic vision of William Joyce afflicts us all but only true art can show us such folly.

One thinks of the other Joyce, as an obvious example of art's humanitarian defence, and of that moment in 'The Dead' when Miss Ivors, the Gaelgóir, gains the upper hand in her conversation with Gabriel Conroy:

> 'And haven't you your own land to visit,' continued Miss Ivors, 'that you know nothing of, your own people, and your own country?'
> 'O, to tell you the truth,' retorted Gabriel suddenly, 'I'm sick of my own country, sick of it!'

Despite her questions as to why this should be so, Gabriel has no answer and avoids, during their dance, the 'sour expression on her face'. 'Then, just as the chain was about to start again, she stood on tiptoe and whispered into his ear: West Briton!'

Gabriel lives in a perpetual state of anxious ambiguity which is easily rankled by Miss Ivors, 'an enthusiast', and by what she stands for in his mind. Gabriel is drawn towards 'Europe' and an imagined style of cultural grace and understanding which he does not see manifest in his own place. Had Miss Ivors, he ponders, 'really any life of her own behind all her propagandism?'

It is a question that underlies much Irish writing since Joyce's time: how can the individual make do in his or her own country, given the moral and cultural conditions that obtain there? It is a question about freedom and choice.

In *Double Cross*, both Brendan Bracken, Minister of Information in Churchill's War Cabinet, and William Joyce, propagandist for Hitlerite fascism, seek to obliterate their past and create, instead, new identities. As Bracken states it:

> I happen to subscribe to the Wildean notion that one must make one's life a work of art. We are given pretty dismal material to start with. One must shape it into significance. I believe that that's what's meant by salvation.

*Double Cross* challenges what Kilroy calls in his 'Author's Note' the 'dangerous absurdity' whereby people base their identity 'exclusively, upon a mystical sense of place rather than in personal character where it properly resides'. The trouble is that both Bracken and Joyce, in time, erase the ground upon which their own characters are based and succumb to caricatures of what they had wished to be: literally, a vicious circle of soul-searching.

Bracken, for instance, variously ascribes to his real father ('a Tipperary stonemason, who was also a dynamite Terrorist', as Joyce dismissively calls him) the identity of 'a bishop, don't you know, on the Cape', 'a distinguished officer in the Indian Army' and 'an admiral'. In a weak moment, Bracken tells Beaverbrook: 'My father had the face of a condemned people.'

Fleeing from that Irish past, Bracken is haunted by images of a forlorn brother which metaphorically underwrite one of the play's most powerful scenes. In the balcony scene just quoted, the present reasserts itself as Bracken recomposes himself. The terror of his loneliness and the absurd distortions he has forced himself through reveal Bracken as a tragically flawed figure. In engineering his rise through English Society, Bracken exhibits a fear of, and contempt for, all that is associated with his past.

When Beaverbrook tells Bracken that he knows the truth about his past, Bracken is appalled, despite Beaverbrook's placations:

Bracken: (Outburst) All that is dead! I want nothing to do with what was! I cannot be what I am if I'm saddled with that.

Beaverbrook: My dear boy, history has been uncommonly generous to you. You should seize upon it as a sign, a charm that few are blessed with. History allowed you to choose. How many more can say the same down the centuries?

Quoting Edmund Burke on 'the British inheritance', Bracken is aghast when Beaverbrook responds by referring to Gandhi:

Bracken: (Sudden turn so that it shocks Beaverbrook and drains Bracken) I don't need to know him. I know his type. That sanctimonious, ascetic face with its watery eyes, running with pious self-denial. Some Peasants in the fields. What an image for the world to imitate! I despise him, begging bowl in one hand, dagger concealed in the other. Determined to prove the superiority of the primitive. I would happily trample him into the ground. What do these people know of law? Of grace? Cultivated living? They would overrun us, mark you. With their foul smells. Their obscene rituals. Animalism.

It is the rhetoric of self-hate that links Bracken to Joyce since, for them both, the ordinary speaks of an ominous, deadly reality.

Like much else in *Double Cross*, with its twinning inversions and mockeries, the scene of Bracken on the balcony is echoed in the second half of the play devoted to Joyce. Joyce is on a rostrum in the semi-darkness before a window, toasting the bombing of Berlin. He is lit by flashes yet, otherwise, there is silence:

(He is drinking heavily throughout) Papa always brought me with him to the Army Barracks in Galway. It was cold in the yard. Two officers were there. Is it quiet in the town, Joyce? Yes, sir. We depend upon men like you, Joyce, to keep the peace. Yes, sir. And who have we here? This is my son, sir. What age are you, boy? Fifteen, sir. And what is your name. William Brooke Joyce. Brooke? Brooke? That, surely, is not an Irish name, is it? His mother's name, sir. Her father was a medical doctor from Ulster. Ah! You are all loyalists in your house, Joyce. Keep up the good work. Then the lorries came in from patrol from the Clifden Road ... The Tans were drunk, but the officers only laughed. We shot some rabbits, one of the Tans shouted. Then Papa went to the Paymaster's Office. Then I ran after the two officers. Just a moment, please! Yes? What is it? Ah, it is young William Joyce. Now, then, speak up. I want to serve, Sir. You want to serve, do you? Yes, Sir.

In his drunken reverie, Joyce swings between the remembered past, with a kind of irrational, pathetic nostalgia, to the rendezvous 'with my great mechanical birds', the English bombers. He refuses to go into the Berlin cellars for safety:

> ... there is a question of fastidiousness. Once our German friend hits the cellar during a raid he produces his sausage. The place reeks of garlic, a compacted offal and broken wind.

But the comedy belies a deeper contempt, what Joyce calls, a little later in the play, the 'rooting out of everything that was common and shabby and second-rate'. Sensing betrayal between his wife Margaret and Erich, a German whom she is teaching English, Joyce turns his belligerent distaste for human contact into a terrifying ordeal of self-doubt and guilt. 'It is the betrayal, the betrayal ...,' he bemoans, before the onslaught of logorrhoeaic abasement:

> Margaret: Please stop. You've talked non-stop for twenty-four hours. We haven't slept. We haven't eaten. We simply cannot go on like this. You must stop talking ... Finally, it stopped. That sickening spill of words. I thought I should never hear that voice stop. But it did. It was like an engine running down. There was always some gap between what he said and what he really felt. When that gap widened all that was left to him was speech. When he stopped talking there was silence for weeks.

Joyce and Bracken are afflicted with 'talk' which compensates for reality and the sense of failure that absurdly tethers them to their Irish past. Language is where they find refuge to live their fantasy lives. Crises come when the 'gap' Margaret refers to seems unbridgeable. This makes *Double Cross* so convincing as tragedy since there is a necessary, inevitable climax to both the characters' misconceptions.

For Bracken, it is when his girlfriend, Popsie, mocks his use of English: 'Well, I must say I have never known anyone to use the English language quite in the way you do, Brendan.'

Bracken: Why not?
Popsie: Well, it's rather as if one were speaking to someone who was discovering the words as he went along. It's aboriginal, extremely refreshing, of course.
Bracken: (He means it) That is the most appalling thing anyone has ever said to me ... You call my use of the language trivial!
Popsie: Of course. One opens one's mouth and words come out. Perfectly straightforward. I should say.
Bracken: It is what makes me what I am! Without it, I am nothing!

So whether it is Bracken performing in the upper reaches of English political and financial circles, or Joyce bawling down the microphone as Lord Haw-Haw, both characters are defined by what they say. There is nothing 'perfectly straightforward' about this, however. They have acquired (even risked), along with their speeches and accents, fictional identities. To shake confidence in one, means a threat to the other. Yet, in their very vulnerability, Bracken and Joyce cast a strange, murky but also chastening, light upon the glum or complacent composure of Beaverbrook, Erich, Popsie, Castlerosse – all those who know their places.

At this point one realises how potent the analogy in *Double Cross* is between Joyce and Bracken on the one hand, and the struggle they embody of an ideal life on the other: the 'perfectibility' of man (for Joyce) and the perfect, cultivated 'English' manner (for Bracken). As Joyce and Bracken are exposed to failure, these ideals are equally exposed. 'What I remember most,' remarks the Lady Journalist who interviews Joyce in his cell shortly before being hanged for treason:

... when justice was done, was not that small, slight man with his ridiculous teutonic bow to the judge, nor the palpable relief of the Londoners that he was not to escape ... What I remember was the group of young fascists, the acolytes, the loyal ones, the young men in the gallery, those pale, blue faces, their dark, shining eyes, that look of inspired poverty, inspired promise. They were weeping. Those lilting Celtic voices in grief at the death of their christus. They put on their old raincoats, like vestments, and talked raucously of patriotism. It was as if they had taken the idea of England to some terrible logical meaning of their own which England itself could never tolerate. And before they left in the rain for some secret meeting, some illicit upper-room, the tears poured down those long, emaciated, Celtic faces. They wept for England.

By chasing down the pathos of these men's lives, *Double Cross* alters the terms by which we can customarily read such things as nationalism, what Kilroy calls 'the whole notion of labelling people according to where they come from'. The play has also restored to the Irish stage the viability of such ideas as having a sustainable theatrical focus. As a play, *Double Cross* is pitched at differently complicated dramatic scales: the stilted farce of Bracken's demeanour; the energetic Players – 'And so, to play!'; the icy stillness in Joyce's retelling of his fatal encounter with two English officers 'in that clearing in the woods' near Wasserleben; the perverse poetry of his vision of man; and the frail tenacity that consumes Bracken when, before the symbols of his England, of Churchill and the King, he reads an unfinished letter:

> Dearest Mother, I have only now been able to reply to your letter. Of course I do understand the pain you feel as you reflect back upon your life. Of course I know how you suffered at the hands of that man, my father, that vicious person. I remember the scenes in Ardvullen House, Mother. I remember all these things, how could I ever forget! But, my dear, he is dead, while you are living. To constantly remind oneself of past unhappiness is to be merely self-indulgent. You must put all that behind you as if it had never happened. Above all, one must utterly reject that which diminishes one, all that betrays one's higher instincts. One's sense of what it is to be civilised is what is important to one. There is nothing else.

What it is to be civilised is the ultimate question which *Double Cross* forces us to keep in mind.

[1987/88]

41

# NORTHERN WINDOWS/
# SOUTHERN STARS

## I

One can get a fair idea of how 'Modern Irish Literature' came into being, reading these diverse and differently enjoyable books: Richard Ellmann's *Four Dubliners*, Frank Ormsby's *Northern Windows* and John Ryan's *Remembering How We Stood*. From Carleton (1794–1869), we move through his rural Ulster aspirations to becoming a Man of Letters in Dublin, via Ellmann's opening chapter on Wilde in 1870s, Oxford and Joyce in Switzerland (1917–19), to the northern voices of John Boyd's Belfast in the 1920s, Ellmann's Yeats in 1934 with his virility problems, and the angles of Greacen, McAughtry and Harbinson on Belfast in the 1930s, before MacNeice's 1941 recollections of his upbringing in County Antrim bring us to the watershed of World War II, where Beckett concludes *Four Dubliners*. During the war and onwards we have, in Ryan's recollections (first published in 1975), Behan, Kavanagh and O'Nolan sequestered in McDaid's bar, while Michael Longley's memory, in *Northern Windows*, spans the late 1930s in Belfast to the present, with the Devlins (Polly and Bernadette) and Robert Johnstone bringing the picture up to the late '50s and early '60s.

Ryan's memoirs, Ormsby's autobiographical selections and Ellmann's recast lectures splice into each other in provocatively contrary ways. The slow embrace of Ryan's sketches contrasts with Ormsby's carefully monitored portrait gallery against which the incisive studies of Ellmann's book perform on a different critical wavelength.

Both Ormsby and Ryan, as editor and memorialist respectively, are affectionate and unassuming in regard to their subjects, although Ryan does force the pace a bit concerning 'reputations' and his being at the centre of things. Ellmann's distance is impeccable.

What emerges from *Four Dubliners* is a cool, objective rendering which shows the individual writers as people of their time. Paradoxically, while being powerfully rooted in one particular place ('Ulster') at various times along a chronological continuum, *Northern Windows* misses the same style of definition, with the uniqueness of the individuals blurring under actual accounts of childhood and growing-up in the province. In some way, we do not actually see more of either the place or the people through *Northern Windows* but, rather, find confirmation of historical realities as we already know them to be. It is a book of reassurance.

*Northern Windows* reveals a kind of unwritten, mutual reserve in which feelings are treated like ideas and ideas turn into family attitudes best not brought out into the open. In a mystifying way, the meaning of sectarianism is not really probed even while it remains the central fact of northern life. Lives are, of course, lived in spite of such a human blight but rarely in these contributions is there a sense of what sectarianism does to everyone concerned. We do not gain any deeper feeling for the kinds of complex emotional and sexual taboos that were, and still are, a basic feature of the religious and social life in the North. This is not a criticism of *Northern Windows* as a book but, rather, of the similar views of the world which emerge from it.

The novelists and poets whose stories largely go to make up *Northern Windows* – Carleton, Shane F. Bullock, Forrest Reid, George Buchanan, Patrick Kavanagh, Louis MacNeice, Sam Hanna Bell, John Boyd, Robert Greacen, Michael Longley and Robert Johnstone – all give entertaining accounts of their past. They read well but we are not – really – hearing the half of it.

In *Remembering How We Stood*, Ryan's reserve proves liberating, yet the candour can lead him into the grand statement, meticulously avoided by all the northerners:

> Writers and artists are endemically quarrelsome; their occupation makes them more distraught and susceptible to hysteria than other professionals; because of art's insecurity and the wounds that the morbidly intelligent inflict upon themselves.

This sounds like hypochondria, the sleeping sickness of the imagination; but is the 'occupation' of being a writer really more prone to hysteria than, say, that of a politician, a dentist, a quantity surveyor, a housewife or football player? The question collapses under the weight of assumption and cliché the contemporary writer must come to terms with concerning both how he or she should act and what he or she is expected to write about. As Ryan says of Behan: 'He seemed to be wired-up to the media.' Public perceptions of poets and poetry are, for instance, generally related to the myth that there is in Ireland 'a standing army' of poets, one of Patrick Kavanagh's 'great' sayings. Even though such a myth can be easily dismissed – by comparison with how many spinsters, retired Yorkshire majors and Cornish rectors are religiously firing off their poems to the literary magazines – it has a life of its own, due mainly to the bland recycling of such 'sayings' of this writer or that as a substitute for genuine criticism.

Hysteria is not, of course, closer to the artist than to any other human being. Artists struggle, often with more failure than success, to embody and carry over into their work pressures of, and upon, the self and throughout society. In Ireland, the problem is our basic uncertainty about the value of the literary work (which standards should we use, for instance? Are there any?), whereas the public role and social occasion of its expression are more readily assimilated as 'stories' and recognised with the standard epithets like 'great' or 'a genius'. This avoids the awkward business of assessing, questioning, considering and vindicating artistic worth, leaving that to anecdote. As with politics in Ireland, personality often means much more, and thence to the ghastly patronage of 'the character'. Louis MacNeice spotted this when he remarked upon the paradox in Joyce, that while 'a master of written dialogue' like Eliot, he remained 'essentially literary and neither of them could be described as a sparkling conversationalist ... It is ironic that the greatest celebrant of Dublin should have been so lacking in the Dubliner's most famous virtue or vice'. The privacy Samuel Beckett maintained is also relevant here.

The bulk of our generalisations about art, writing and the imagination, reflects this distinct critical unease. So the poet must 'suffer' and be seen to suffer: Kavanagh in his miserable Dublin bachelor flat is an identifiable image, whereas Joyce, attended by friends and well-wishers in a French apartment, is not. The price of recognition is perceived somewhere between priest (vocation) and vagabond (dislocation); reverence with piety, a fateful mix at the best of times. The cost this exacts as regards reality is colossal, yet Irish writers have been prone to accept these terms, petulantly but inevitably; or else fly the coop, as many from Wilde's time on have indeed done. Ellmann's chapter on Samuel Beckett, for example, records that:

> At the age of twenty-two Beckett went from Dublin to Paris; twenty-six years before, at the age of twenty, Joyce made the same journey. Equally pivotal were the displacements of Yeats at twenty-two from Dublin to London, and of Wilde, at twenty, from Dublin to Oxford. The geographical change symbolised for all four of them an attempt to proceed from the known to the unknown, to remake themselves in unfamiliar air.

There is, too, a telling moment in Louis MacNeice's autobiography, *The Strings Are False*, when in 1939, having travelled around the west of Ireland and heard in Galway the news of the outbreak of war, he spends a final few days in Dublin:

> ... I was alone with the catastrophe, spent Saturday drinking in a bar with Dublin literati; they hardly debated the war but debated the correct versions of Dublin street songs ... The intelligentsia continued their parties, their mutual malice was as effervescent as ever. There was still a pot of flowers in front of Matt Talbot's shrine, the potboy priests and the birds of prey were still the dominant caste; the petty bureaucracy continued powerful and petty.

It was during this period – the late 1930s to the mid-1950s

– that some popular images of poets and poetry took root in Ireland. Possibly because poets were prominent in the struggle that achieved the political and economic independence of the Irish Free State from the British Empire, their profile has remained consistently more visible than, say, that of playwrights, novelists or visual artists. However, if one takes the four Dubliners of Richard Ellmann's book (Wilde, Yeats, Joyce and Beckett), we do not associate them with either the 'hysteria' Ryan sees as the hallmark of writers or, in their maturity, as being denizens of Dublin 'literati' pub-life.

The public perception of these four people is as artists. While these perceptions may be shaded by Wilde's homosexuality, Yeats' love affair with Maud Gonne and his presumed arrogance, Joyce's exiled 'love-hate' relationship with the country or Beckett's remoteness and 'obscure' plays, their acknowledgement remains as artists.

This is a complicated business, better left for another occasion. When we turn to Behan, O'Nolan and Kavanagh, the three Dublin-based writers who figure in *Remembering How We Stood*, we read of a demonstrative yet repressed existence in which drink plays the dominant part – of seemingly opening doors to a freer life, while effectively encouraging the delusion that things can be different without imaginative (and political) struggle for real change.

The men of John Ryan's book (women rarely feature) are caught between heroes and ideals on the one hand and, on the other, the country as it was in the 1940s and '50s, closed off from the world, maintaining a phoney diplomatic status quo which, afterwards, slumped into the deplorable exodus of people in search of a decent standard of living elsewhere after the war (or 'the Emergency' as it was known in 'the Free State').

The writers who remained in Ireland during this time had their work cut out for them but, as Ryan's memoirs recall, they were part of a wider supportive community, albeit a literary one. For Denis Devlin, Brian Coffey, Samuel Beckett, even Sean O'Faoláin, Francis Stuart and Louis MacNeice, their separateness wrote them out of the Irish literary 'scene' and, largely, continues to do so.

In *Remembering How We Stood*, John Ryan, having established the mood of the time, accords to his friends a heroism of sorts:

> ... We shared the experience of working together in besieged times when the worst enemy was the one within the gates. They were the keepers of the nation's conscience ...

I dare say Joyce would have had none of this, even though it is down to his creation that we must forge the uncreated conscience of the race. Stephen Dedalus, however, was a very idealistic young man. According to Ellmann, Joyce wanted ordinary men and women

> ... to know themselves as they really were, not as they were taught by church and state to be. He gave dignity to the common life that we all share.

It is this dignity which a writer can harm most because it is his own but, stripped of the sense of having a place in common with his peers, a shared life, the writer eventually reacts against that society in whatever way is the most accessible and meaningful to it. All too often in Ireland, 'drink' has been that symbolic gesture of rejection – rejecting the self, the home, the marriage, the restrictions of life, real or imagined. It is hardly stretching the point to see Behan, Kavanagh and Brian O'Nolan as victims of this particular cultural malaise, in parallel with Hemingway, Fitzgerald and Berryman.

Since 1967, when Kavanagh died, some things have, of course, changed. As Thomas Kilroy remarked in his essay 'The Irish Writer: Self and Society, 1950–80':

> The public position of a Seamus Heaney, a John McGahern, a Brian Friel is manifestly different to that of a Brian Coffey, a Patrick Kavanagh, a Brinsley MacNamara. The change has to do with the earnestness, the sometimes gauche and embarrassing earnestness, with which the Irish public in these decades has strained towards its particular conception of modernity.

Homing in on Kavanagh as representative, Kilroy describes him stalking 'through the fifties like some *cainteoir* [vagrant satirist] out of the Gaelic past with that sartorial stamp, the swinging coat, the dipped brooding hat, the notorious cough and splutter, arms akimbo, knotted like an embrace that has lost or crushed its loved object'. 'It will be the business of the biographer,' Kilroy concludes, 'to analyse the kind of distortions of selfhood which Kavanagh affected in his role as a poet and to question the kind of society which impelled him, often with great cruelty and delight in the histrionics, towards a perverse form of self-satisfaction on the part of society itself.'

It is a society still with us today, even though the strain towards modernity has split into two, with increasingly more people struggling to keep their heads above water while a privileged few gain near-total access to monetary wealth and its cultural trimmings.

## II

Circumstances have, however, all too often led us into a rigid force of habit, detached from what is actually going on in Irish society. In this regard, Sarah Nelson, in her book *Ulster's Uncertain Defenders* (1984), makes a simple but crucial point:

> Conflicts and solutions are played out by real people; to examine their feelings and experiences is to restate the importance of people, not as pawns in a historical process but as actors who respond to and influence events.

Over the years Ireland, North and south, has come in for an exorbitant amount of attention. Writers have been urged to become guru-like figures addressing 'historical problems'; talking about themselves and their work is now an expected element in Irish writing. Somehow, though, the sharp edge of criticism, the exploration of the structure and contemporary meaning of a writer's work, has blurred into a 'themey' mist. Reality – what is happening and why – is shunted off into an adjunct of writing, like an afterthought.

Yet the central facts of life in Ireland remain: the eruption and continuation for a quarter of a century of political upheaval in Northern Ireland, matched by deep-seated social, moral and sexual tensions and resentments in the Republic. 'The Troubles' are unquestionably the watershed in recent Irish history. Life changed irrevocably, both directly and indirectly, for hundreds of thousands, including my own generation, who inherited ordinary hopes in the future only to see these break up in the grim squalor of daily bombings and nightly assassinations. A wedge has been driven into the emotional life of that generation, between the past of the 1960s, when they were teenagers, and the present.

This rupture in time made many exiles from their own youth, forcing them to look back, sometimes with nostalgia but, more often, with unflinching realism, to a time never allowed its chance. This sense of incompleteness will, I imagine, haunt many of us for the rest of our days. It has put paid to the assumption that life is a natural, linear process. As Czeslaw Milosz said in *The Captive Mind*:

> Man tends to regard the order he lives in as natural. The houses he passes on his way to work seem more like rocks rising out of the earth than products of human hands. He considers the work he does in his office or factory as essential to the harmonious functioning of the world ... His first stroll along a street littered with glass from bomb-shattered windows, shakes his faith in the 'naturalness' of his world.

With that realisation, the certainties also go. For the writers, it involves trying to remake connections between words and things within verifiable experience and not what these have been made (or assumed) to represent in the past.

It is refreshing, therefore, to read John Hewitt, who did not loll around in our hang-ups but got on with the job and kept his eye (perhaps too much so) on what was literally going on around him. Hewitt states in *Ancestral Voices* (1987):

> The careful rejection of the rhetorical and flamboyant, the stubborn concreteness of the imagery, the conscientious cleaving to objects of sense which, not at all paradoxically, provides the best basis and launching ground for the lonely ascents of practical mysticism which lie close to the heart of Ulster's best intellectual activity and make us bold enough to claim Concord as a townland of our own.

This single-mindedness meant that Hewitt rarely let caricature and received opinion get in the way of what he needed to say. Hewitt was, after all, a committed man who held to certain ideas, like regionalism, and beliefs, like socialism, throughout his life. These ideas, particularly his socialism, cost him dearly. Not surprisingly, they are the mainstays of *Ancestral Voices: The Selected Prose of John Hewitt*, sometimes explicitly so, though often unvoiced. The even-tempered manner of Hewitt's prose describes an attitude to the world which is always instructive:

> ... by the mid-1920s, with the new ministries in gear and the non-entities trooping to the Westminster backbenches, it seemed evident that the Unionists were a right wing offshoot of the British Tory Party, who at home fought every election on the border, and that the Nationalists, the representatives of the Catholic minority, were merely obsolete clansmen with old slogans, moving in an irrelevant dream, utterly without the smallest fig-leaf of a social policy.

As well as calling the political shots, *Ancestral Voices* doubles back to a real question which, curiously, casts doubt upon the very entity which Hewitt is credited with creating – the Ulster Writer.

> The Ulster ideology then offered the writer no inspiration. The Ulster public offered him no livelihood. Nor has the latter problem yet been solved. There must be very few writers who can be entirely dependent on writing, as apart from journalism, in the whole Irish island. Hence the writer is confronted with another highly personal question: how to make his art not merely an escape-mechanism or recreation from his routine avocation: how to make his daily work provide a flow of experience usable in his art; or, at least, how to ensure that the nature and the demands of his calling do not smother his aesthetic sensibilities. These each must solve for himself but they can have their profitable side. Until he has absorbed a deal of human experience no man is fit to write anything of value. If writers in an isolated group or in individual segregation are for too long disassociated from the social matrix their work will inevitably grow thin and tenuous, more and more concerned with form rather than content, heading for marvellous feats of empty virtuosity.

Behind the unassuming bearing of Hewitt the writer, one also senses restlessness and a probing self-consciousness.

Hewitt well understood poetry as a powerful compensation for the inadequacies of the social reality which he had inherited and sought to transform; the personal life imaginatively subdued, knowing its place in the scheme of things. Therein lies the struggle which Hewitt's writing represents against a collective inertia buried deep in the past, in his ancestral voices. It gives his writing an unforced edge of grace and constraint but, always, the humility of the true artist.

As Tom Clyde, the editor of *Ancestral Voices*, remarks, Hewitt's prose was 'driven by a need to define himself in terms of the past, both of his family and of his province, to dig out long-buried artists and rebels, to trace lines of descent, to forge his own personal mythology'. This most honourable of men looked all around and saw what he thought could civilise. In a sense, his work can be summed up by Robert Lowell's description of Frost as a poet who 'somehow put life into a dead tradition'. What Hewitt's mythology actually meant in terms of his own life, art and times awaits the critical biographer. In the interim, *Ancestral Voices* restates the importance of John Hewitt to all the people from whom he came and carries his emphatic rebuke to those who see themselves as pawns in an inevitable historical process:

> We have had enough of the rigid clichés of stubborn politicians, the profit-focused intensity of men of business, the dogmatic arrogance of the Churches, the intolerance of sectarians, the lack of human sympathy of the doctrinaire, of all those whose ready instinct is for violence in word and act.

And, perhaps, this is where the trouble starts – in the divergent and contradictory Irish senses of being a citizen or, more directly, of the definition of civic space to which individuals are responsible, beyond immediate demands of home, family and religion.

In his fine novel, *The Death Of Men* (1981), set in Italy during the abduction and assassination of Aldo Moro, the Scottish writer Allan Massie has his chief character, Raimundo, remark:

> ... when I thought about it [a hanging] the rough Justice of the Partisans had done nothing to prepare Italians for civil life: if we contrived to tear ourselves apart, wasn't it to some extent at least because of the honour we accorded to that violence we had decided to commemorate?

Irish life is similarly afflicted – 'the honour we accorded to that violence we had decided to commemorate'. Behind the influential, prim decorum of English law, the northern Unionists, for instance, were willing and able to maintain a little feudal state of their own, self-righteously convinced that their masters in London had been more than well-paid, from the rows of ships that slid off the slipways to the dutiful generations that fought the wars and died in their thousands. Now, of course, all that is changed, as indeed it had to, since the North was built as a state upon such precarious foundations. It is grimly tragic, though, that it took so long to recognise this.

While the Republic mesmerises itself with a post-industrial boom based upon foreign capital and international financial services, the currents of change, North and south, will finally begin to surface and find their own level. As Raimundo remarks:

> It is the State, not the family, which exists as the means of guarding civil life; and that is, after all, what we mean by civilisation. It is a product of the State. Without the sanction of the State, we are back in the days of the robber barons. Isn't this what Aquinas meant by his justification of the State, that, for fallen man, it is the sine qua non of civil life?

So much writing about life in Ireland and so many lives of Irish writers, in this as in previous generations, have been haunted by that very question.

[1987–1989]

# THE SOUND OF THE SHUTTLE

## I

The city we inhabit is a dream
And visions all her streets and all her towers ...
                  – Richard Rowley, 'City Dawn'

When John Keats went on a walking visit of Ireland in 1818, his impression of Belfast, like his overall sense of 'the rags, dirt and misery of the poor common Irish' was far from dreamlike:

> We heard on passing into Belfast through a most wretched suburb that most disgusting of all noises, worse than the bagpipe, the laugh of a monkey, the chatter of women solus, the scream of a macaw – I mean the sound of the shuttle. What a tremendous difficulty is the improvement of the condition of such people.

Since that time, Belfast has been identified as an industrial centre unsympathetic to the romantic imaginative spirit that a poet such as John Keats personified. If the linen-shuttle has disappeared, to be replaced by the commuter-belt airplane, the afterglow of Belfast's industrial past persists. Time and time again, in the literature of the past two centuries and more, if and when Belfast is mentioned, it is as a town engrossed in commerce and hardened by the graft of industrialism. A city, that is, condemned, or at least disdained, for its lack of imaginative offspring or feeling for things literary. In *The Oxford Literary Guide to the British Isles* (1977), Belfast's 'literary connections' are defined as being 'mainly with those writers who were born here, but there is a dearth of monuments or places of pilgrimage'. That there could be 'a dearth of monuments' in such a monumentalised city as Belfast seems incredible but the authors, Dorothy Eagle and Hilary Carnell, are probably correct about the 'places of pilgrimage' simply because Belfast, until comparatively recently, has usually been considered indifferent to the creation of art and literature. What I would like to do here is make some comments about the possible reasons why this should be so.

Little has been written about Belfast that is not a political, economic, statistical or sociological study and even the religious studies seem humdrum inspections. My feeling is that critics, literary and cultural, have stayed away from looking at Belfast simply because it seemed a dour, unimpressive cousin to the cosmopolitan flamboyance of Dublin and that, fraught as it may well be with bloody themes, the romance of Dublin's 20th-century history shines marvellously in comparison with the monotonous siren of the half-baked and surly northern city. This was to change, of course, in the late '60s and '70s when Belfast shot to world prominence as a political flashpoint, but the old-style caricature lasted like an iron mould. It was, and to some extent still is, a cast fixed in the hegemony of Protestantism, and even while no such cultural edifice exists, the influence of Protestantism in all its manifestations has determined the city's sense of itself.

Indeed, it is all very well for Geoffrey Bell, in his book *The Protestants of Ulster* (1978), to talk of 'the Protestant way of life' through quotations from *Loyalist News* or *Orange Cross* and declare: 'That is what the Protestant culture is all about: Protestant supremacy, Protestant ascendency', but he comes no closer to understanding 'the Protestant way of life' than any hostile nationalist. Instead, he merely sneers at it, ignoring the fact that the aspects he concentrates on (the songs, the football, the work) could, with qualifications, be applied to working-class communities throughout these islands. The ascendency (or supremacy) of Protestantism is the key to understanding what is all too obvious in cultural terms regarding Belfast: namely, its restricted and suspicious sense of 'culture' as a natural aspect of individual and social experience.

In *Culture and Anarchy in Ireland 1890–1939* (1979), F. S. L. Lyons tackles the issue in some depth: he talks about this 'simple culture' as being 'for most of its adherents, a non-literary one which did not encourage either reading or the writing of imaginative literature'.

So, while there are various poetic works towards the end of the 18th century (like those of Bishop Percy of Dromore) and the rural folk poetry chronicled by John Hewitt, the 19th century of William Allingham leads silently, lamely, towards Louis MacNeice:

> Few novels, little poetry, hardly any drama, attract the eye until the beginning of the twentieth century. This was not due so much to lack of talent, as to lack of interest and, more particularly, to lack of patronage.

I am not sure that if Sir Edward Harland had cast his mind and money around we would have had a poet's or playwright's statue adorning the phalanx of the City Hall in the place of, say, Lord Dufferin, but the idea is intriguing all the same. What seems more to the point is when Lyons connects, implicitly, this cultural 'void' with the 'Protestant myth'. Here we are on solid ground.

As Lyons narrates, Presbyterianism, particularly in the east Ulster countryside, paved the way, through English and Scottish craftsmen and weavers of the 17th century, towards an accumulation of capital which, in turn, was converted during the 19th century into entrepreneurial power and prestige, a status of domineering influence throughout the business, social and cultural life of Belfast. It was this class (counterparts to the later emergent Catholic middle class which Yeats came to despise) that imposed its own order on the unruly instability of modern Belfast.

Like all myths, in other words, the Protestant myth was a constructed one which some employed for amassing huge profits, while the majority of others (passively, sometimes militantly) supported it for their own protection and incremental advancement. Translated into an act of faith, this myth, as Lyons points out, 'appealed to religious primitivism, but it also provided colour, poetry and its own kind of magic for ordinary drab lives'. The problem has always been why this 'magic' is transformed into the nightmare of bigotry and sectarianism: those 'deep reserves of emotion which the normal conduct of their religion kept in strict restraint, but which, largely because of that restraint, could build up from time to time into explosions of violent feelings and actions'.

John Wilson Foster may have indirectly uncovered one of the reasons for this transformation from magic into violence when he remarked, in his *Forces and Themes in Ulster Fiction* (1974):

> If the stereotype is to be believed, Protestants exhibit a narrower emotional range and a greater, more careful and, on the whole, less imaginative stability, a stability that owes itself to their Protestant religion, the mythless recency of their Irishness, and their Scottish patrimony.

There is an important frame of reference being formulated here which places the Protestant myth in a new and possibly creative perspective. For if the stereotype is believed as a paradigm, without any loss of face but as an acknowledgement of historical facts, how these facts – of plantation, battle, massacre, victory – become integrated and related to political analysis and opinion is secondary to the way they are translated into imaginative or cultural terms. They become, that is, sources of reference which clarify identity rather than counters of belief which threaten identity, as so often happens. It is this latter effect which will, according to Foster:

> ... reinforce the Protestants' unflattering self-concept and make them strengthen the psychic walls that not only protect but also confine and inhibit. For the Ulster Protestant who is conscious of his heritage and is not merely a peripheral Englishman, this self-consciousness is creatively crippling.

Or not as the case may be, since Foster and Lyons do not consider that the Protestant myth can become a source of imaginative strength as much as one of imaginative debility. Similarly, Belfast has more recently become a critical influence on the development of culture (primarily literary) in Ireland, rather than the Medusa it was conveniently taken to be. In the years ahead, this 'Protestant Myth' will hopefully find itself less under the perplexed gaze of the shocked troops of British and Irish liberalism but seen more for what it is.

Again, perhaps Lyons has anticipated this possible shift when he talks of 'the dualism of militant Protestantism', that residue of historical imperatives he describes elsewhere in his book, with its visible contrasts such as those found in the July 12th celebrations. Between the 'brilliant barbarity of the setting, its noise and glitter' and the 'sobriety of the serried ranks of grim, serious and utterly respectable marchers' one finds, in Prof. Lyons' terms, 'a formidable juxtaposition': the 'immobility and the dynamism of Protestant culture which mingles resolution and hysteria, siege and deliverance in a volatile dialectic'. One need only consider Lyons' use of the word 'hysteria' to disclose the intimate range and depth of Protestant feeling. For as 'they' see it, Belfast is 'their' city, the birthplace which has been terribly maltreated. Hence we find the recurrent dream of deliverance from this desperate situation. But deliverance means not only 'setting free'; it also means 'a giving up' or 'giving over', almost a 'surrendering'. It is against this reading that the other two psychologies come to bear: of siege and resolution, the steeling of an army and the maintenance of its absolute vigilance.

These seemingly hectic gyrations of feeling can be likened to the cacophonous movement of Keats' shuttle, drowning out the personal voice of imaginative expression.

Unquestionably, after much pain and delusion, Protestants are coming to the realisation, induced by the changing attitudes of the English establishment, that they must reconsider their own past, not as a gesture of 'Sell Out' or 'Compromise', but simply to know themselves better and also to know what the future may hold. In this angry, inarticulate and bloody process, Keats' elevated opening to the first version of *The Fall of Hyperion*, written around the same time as his experience of Ireland, has a telling ring to it:

> Fanatics have their dreams, wherewith they weave
> A paradise for a sect; the savage, too,
> From forth the loftiest fashion of his sleep

Guesses at heaven; pity these have not
Traced upon vellum or wild Indian leaf
The shadows of melodious utterance,
But bare of laurel they live, dream, and die;
For Poesy alone can tell her dreams, –
With the fine spell of words alone can save
Imagination from the sable chain
And dumb enchantment. Who alive can say,
'Thou art no Poet – mays't not tell thy dreams?'
Since every man whose soul is not a clod
Hath visions and would speak, if he had loved,
And been well nurtured in his mother tongue.

## II

Just how the 'Protestant' community 'hath visions and would speak' is difficult to imagine, given the depth of prejudice that has characterised its sense of being a community at odds with the rest of the country in which it lives. My own experience might be relevant here. Having spent many years uncritically accepting the caricatures of the Protestant North from which I came, it was only after I had left Belfast that I started to explore the feelings, beliefs, attitudes, experiences and history of the Protestants in that part of Ireland. It was a strange sensation of uncovering, under the layers of bigotry, delusion and uncertainty, the human relation of the Protestants to their own past. Even while I still stood (and stand today) politically outside and critical of that relationship, I realised that nothing would ever materially change unless people started from the human story rather than the theoretical premise. What's more, as someone who writes poems, the crux of the matter was that I knew I could achieve a kind of imaginative coherence for myself only if I looked deeper at how my Protestant upbringing had influenced me. This meant looking at that background and examining its cultural and literary expression in the Ireland of today. My feeling is that poems should speak for themselves, and that poets should let their poetry do just that, so I will not be referring to my own except at the conclusion of this essay.

Instead, I want to take a look at what the term 'Protestant imagination' can possibly mean in a few literary examples. My choice is, it must be stressed, a highly selective one.

Two illustrations might prove useful as a way of focusing the theme. The first is from A.T.Q. Stewart's *The Ulster Crisis: Resistance to Home Rule 1912–1914*:

> The climax of Covenant Day came when Carson left the Ulster Club to go on board the Liverpool steamer. The docks were only a few minutes' walk away, but it took an hour for the wagonette, drawn not by horses but by men, to reach its destination. More than 70,000 people had managed to jam themselves into Castle Place, all of them intent upon getting near enough to shake Carson's hand, and at the quayside they would not let him go. 'Don't leave us', they shouted. 'You mustn't leave us'. Then at last he got on board the steamer, aptly named the *Patriotic*, they called for yet another speech from him as he stood in the beam of a searchlight at the rail of the upper deck. He left them with the message they never tired of hearing and promised to come back, if necessary to fight. Then as the steamer cast off he heard the vast crowd in the darkness begin to sing 'Rule Britannia' and 'Auld Lang Syne' and then 'God Save the King', and as she moved into the channel rockets burst in red, white and blue sparks above her, and bonfires sprang up on either shore of the Lough.

The second image is much less theatrical but it involves the same figure – Lord Carson. I am not, let me say clearly, interested here in Carson's character but in the way he reflects the contrary states of 'Protestantism' in its political guise of unionism and, as this second example dramatises, the generally accepted notion of the Protestant attitude to the 'imagination'.

Even though both attended Trinity College, a world of difference separates Oscar Wilde from his peer, Edward Carson. Though they went their own ways, fate or whatever it is that tumbles us one direction instead of another, drew them together again. Let me refer to A.T.Q. Stewart's book *Edward Carson* (1981):

> Carson had been crossing the Strand one day when he was almost knocked down by a fine carriage drawn by two horses. The carriage stopped and out stepped Carson's old college contemporary, Oscar Wilde. Wilde was at the very height of his fame as a playwright and a literary lion in London society, one whose witticisms were

attentively gathered and repeated in drawing-rooms throughout the country. He had become plump and prosperous; his countenance bore all the marks of high living and self-indulgence, and he was flamboyantly attired, exhibiting a white carnation in his buttonhole. 'Hullo, Ned Carson. How are you?' he said affably, stretching out his hand, which Carson shook. 'Fancy you being a Tory and Arthur Balfour's right-hand man! You're coming along, Ned. Come and dine with me one day in Tite Street'. Carson had never liked Wilde, but he was touched by his friendliness. Had he accepted the invitation, Wilde's tragic history might have been different, for it was Carson's strict rule never to appear against anyone from whom he had accepted hospitality. The brief which Russell now offered him was to defend the Marquess of Queensberry against a charge of criminal libel and the prosecution had been initiated by Wilde.

The exchanges between these two men – both Irish Protestants – reveal something which it is important to grasp and relate to that other image involving Carson. There is a critical turn in the cross-examination where Carson, defending the Marquess of Queensberry, begins doggedly to undermine Wilde's confidence and studied flippancy:

> The climax of this remarkable cross-examination was reached when Carson asked Wilde about a boy called Grainger, who was Lord Alfred Douglas's servant in Oxford. 'Did you kiss him?' Carson asked. For one fatal moment Wilde's quick wits deserted him. 'Oh dear, no,' he replied without thinking. 'He was a peculiarly plain boy. He was, unfortunately, extremely ugly. I pitied him for it.' Carson pounced like a tiger. Was that the reason Wilde had never kissed him? Suddenly Wilde was on the verge of breaking down. 'Oh, Mr. Carson, you are pertinently insolent'. But Carson continued his remorseless questions. 'You sting me and insult me and try to unnerve me and at times one says things flippantly when one ought to speak more seriously. I admit it.' At this Carson gathered together his papers and sat down.

Wilde is defeated but it is only the beginning of the end for him. Within three years, he was dead. Meanwhile, Carson received much congratulations for his handling of the case and, though reserved in his moment of triumph, he obviously took pleasure in his success. As Stewart has it:

> The sun-god [Wilde] had fallen abruptly to earth, humbled by the plodding contemporary [Carson] he had tried to patronise.

These are, in my mind, two acts which dramatise the Protestant imagination in Ireland. For if we had 70,000 Protestants, some of whom had actually physically drawn Carson's carriage on that day in 1912, their pleading to him to stay suggests a desperate need, a sense of being fatherless, leaderless and hero-less. In that situation, the unlikely figure of Carson becomes their Liberator. Earlier, in 1895, he had proved his powers of advocacy in destroying the dandified Wilde and now he is the reluctant host of Fortune.

Some may baulk at the very notion of hero-worship but the fact of the matter is that such figures as Carson did, to many Protestants, represent a freedom, an identity being confirmed, or to put this in slightly different terms he represented an imaginative focus, a dramatising of themselves through his portrayal as the austere, uncompromising, rigid protector of 'Truth'. That this image should be established during a crucial period in Irish history (the 1890s and 1910s) underlies what I think both examples tell us about the Protestant imagination in Ireland. Because it was effectively from this time, just prior to World War I, that the Protestants in the North became increasingly more isolated from the rest of the country, whilst those living in what is now the Republic had to choose what political or cultural grounds they would define themselves by: Irish, Anglo-Irish, English, British. Eventually, marooned within their own statelet, the Protestants of the North had no other source of imaginative stability than the unexplored, hasty formulation of a Carson, who was, as the second example shows, not only unsympathetic to the exaggerated, aesthetic decadence of a Wilde, but totally incapable of seeing beneath its surface. The possibility, then, of an alternative imaginative tradition being 'officially' sanctioned or even fostered in the North, as was the case in the Republic, was most unlikely. Whatever creative springs there were could be tapped only by the populist displays of mass demonstrations, pacts and sacred covenants, dogmatically separated from the historical developments of the rest of the country. Until, that is, the poet John Hewitt started to bind the wounds and seek (tentatively) an imaginative détente with his peers in the rest of Ireland from the late '30s onwards.

But I do not want to list those occasions, either in the twentieth century or in earlier ones, when Protestants from the North and the south made effective efforts to absorb and transform 'Irish Culture' into their own image. I want, instead, to consider the phrase 'Protestant imagination' and ask if such a thing exists in the first place.

If we accept that, with a personality like Carson so influential in the formation of 'modern' Protestant unionist ideology (and with men like James Craig about to follow), it was unlikely that the state formed out of that ideology would foster an imaginative literary tradition – then we should consider the response elsewhere in Ireland and what better place than in Yeats' poems and those published in *Responsibilities* (1914). This volume is a central one in Yeats because it marks a change of tone – the poems become starker and more realistic; they question the dreamy Celticism of his previous work and turn, often with bitterness, upon the nationalist leaders of a cause Yeats had long espoused (independence from England and the fostering of a national literature) but which he saw turning into narrow dogma. *Responsibilities* records his disillusionment. 'September 1913', a key poem in the collection, is unmistakable in its attitude of scorn, bred of disenchantment with a dream (a tendency, we note, he seemed unable to check in himself since later he was to bay with the dogs of fascism):

> Was it for this the wild geese spread
> The grey wing upon every tide;
> For this that all that blood was shed,
> For this Edward Fitzgerald died,
> And Robert Emmet and Wolfe Tone,
> All that delirium of the brave?
> Romantic Ireland's dead and gone,
> It's with O'Leary in the grave.

Romantic Ireland had 'died and gone' in Yeats' mind and, in registering this, Yeats, who had helped create 'Romantic

Ireland', touches upon one of the common elements of the 'Protestant' imagination – its insistence on measuring Irish dream against Irish reality and a reluctance to embrace what is often seen as an impoverished reality. (It took James Joyce to accept and celebrate that.) The great dream of a united culture, of a people actively committed to literary ideals, broke up under the pressure of actual political manoeuvring and the material needs of an ascendant and deeply conservative middle class. Yeats records this disillusionment as an activist, as one who worked tirelessly in promoting cultural idealism. In stark contrast, Samuel Beckett started off, in *More Pricks Than Kicks* and *Murphy*, from that point of disillusionment, made fun of it and debunked the entire notion of an Irish literary culture united, one and all. Then he left the country for good.

In Beckett, we find an avoidance of nationalism and any other 'ism' or generalisation such as Protestant, which he sees as limiting the deeper search for personal identity. His Dublin Protestant middle-class background, however, guaranteed an isolation which attendance at the Trinity College of the late 1920s only confirmed. This suggests a second characteristic of the Protestant imagination – of having to think about one's cultural position, of being literally 'self-conscious'. Beckett represents the perfect example of an artist who, because of his background, is from the outset forced to question his own identity. In a way, his work parallels the actual historic situation of Protestants in Ireland. For, surely, that painful process of finding out 'What we are' characterises the present state of northern Protestants? Yet many are frightened of accepting that question and hide behind the loudest preacher; others are prepared to face the uncertainty of the time or else leave it all behind them and emigrate.

For the Protestant lack of a 'recognised' cultural home (there is, after all, no such thing as British literature) has created a sense of displacement which inspires the excessive proclaiming 'We are British'. (The situation is, of course, much more complicated than I am making out and for a comprehensive examination of this question of identity, David

Millar's *Queen's Rebels: Ulster Loyalism in Historical Perspective* (1978) is excellent.)

The further twist in this distorted and distorting process of identity is the way the Protestant community in the North of Ireland is seen as an introverted, imaginatively dull and uncreative source for an artist or writer. One need only think of how often the place has been characterised as 'dour' and even the 'black' of the Black North seems to blank out all possibility of imaginative light. To challenge this crippling stereotype would also be to question fundamentally foreign perceptions of Ireland and the Irish as wild and imaginative, tripping over themselves with frothy language. More importantly, it might make the Irish reconsider their own self-image in cultural and political terms.

The third and last writer to whom I will refer has led many readers and critics to make these very necessary reconsiderations. Belfast-born poet Derek Mahon reveals in his work a critical understanding of the Protestant community. It is as though, at long last, Oscar Wilde is turning the tables on Edward Carson. The small poem 'Nostalgias' (originally called 'The Chair Squeaks') defines that sense of aloneness which many see as fundamental to both the Protestant community and also the 'Protestant' writer:

> The chair squeaks in a high wind,
> Rain falls from its branches;
> The kettle yearns for the mountain
> The soap for the sea.
> In a tiny stone church
> On a desolate headland
> A lost tribe is singing 'Abide With Me'.

'A lost tribe': if such is what the Protestant community is, then the poets whose roots are sunk in that community are probing where the real world is (and not the one so many want to believe is the real one – of a Glorious Empire and deliverance from hordes of marauding fenians!) and making it possible, imaginatively, for others to begin to see their horizons and different possibilities.

In many of Mahon's poems, a mirror is held up in which the northern Protestant community can see itself. In the unflattering conclusion to 'Ecclesiastes', he comes closer to understanding the nature of that community than any other poet I know:

> Your people await you, their heavy washing
>    flaps for you in the housing estates –
> a credulous people. God, you could do it, God
>    help you, stand on a corner stiff
> with rhetoric, promising nothing under the sun.

While in a poem like 'Going Home', originally 'The Return', too long to quote satisfactorily here, an appropriate symbol is created of the tenacious spirit that so often cripples northern Protestants instead of inspiring their confidence in the necessity and management of change:

> Rooted in stony ground,
> A last stubborn growth
> Battered by constant rain
> And twisted by the sea-wind
>
> With nothing to recommend it
> But its harsh tenacity ...

Of course, reading a poem will never subdue a bigot or dissolve the political divisions inherited from sectarian attitudes. It might, however, open the door on history, the individual's place in it, the willing and frank acknowledgement of what has been done in their name and the possibility thereby of transforming this experience into a sustaining creative one. The choice is clear: either this is achieved or the myths that northern Protestants live by will petrify further into fear, hatred and the self-disgust that goes with the debilitation of what is their greatest strength – their historical will. Only then can a proper dialogue begin between the different traditions in the whole country. As Joseph Campbell remarked in *The Masks of God*, 'the opening, that is to say, of one's own truth and depth to the depth and truth of another in such a way as to establish an authentic community of existence'.

I am only too aware of the obstacles standing in the way of such a genuine community being built, and personal images swarm in suggesting just how entrenched the resistance is to attaining it – from the crowd of Protestant women spitting upon and then attacking a lonely Catholic motorcyclist during the 'Constitutional Stoppage' of 1974 to the macabre and brutish acts inflicted in the name of a 'Protestant way of life' upon those of the other side.

It was partially an attempt to transcend these scenes, and many others like them, that led me to write 'Seamen's Mission', a poem about something I remembered when, as a child, I stood isolated for a moment in the abstract gloom after a Sunday morning's church service. Belfast receded and 'History' came to the fore:

> The high dome sticks out in my mind
> as the Minister kneads the pulpit's bow
> ferrying us through treacherous oceans.
> Outside the sun dabbles and in the beams
> of stained-glass dust radiates from nowhere
> to the vaulted dreams of our departed,
> heads uplifted under royal flags
> and conquering psalms of the spirit.
>
> The girls fidget and the elders adjust themselves
> for the final half-hour.
> *Let the bells ring out, we who praise Hope*
> *will stand together in stone-cold portals*
> *blinking with the light.*

That entering into reality, from the colonial past to the bequeathed present of 'conquering psalms', that 'blinking with the light', is what the imagination can achieve. It is meaningless to describe such a movement as being either 'Protestant' or 'Catholic'. The shedding of those terms is, instead, the factual condition of any imagination but it would be dishonest to suggest that the getting rid of them is solely the imagination's task. Far from it. Only when an individual's imagination unsolicitedly expresses the experience of the Protestant community will that community, with time, be able to see itself freely. To accomplish this is, however, only part of the artist's responsibility which is, primarily, to be truthful to one's self and writing. For too long, this has meant in Ireland an impotent personal disengagement, an inward complaint; the imagination's equivalent of 'a curse on all your houses'; the bitterness of division rather than the ferment of difference; the promotion of cultural dogmas and decayed ideals, instead of the excitement of experiment and self-discovery. A rigorous art, in other words.

[1983]

# TELLING A STORY

I want to discuss a book I edited in 1985 with the literary critic Edna Longley, called *Across a Roaring Hill: The Protestant Imagination in Modern Ireland*. My approach will be mostly informal, moving back and forth between these points of reference, drawing upon my own personal story as someone who comes from a Belfast Protestant background and who reacted very negatively against that background until comparatively recently when I started to question, with a more constructive critical eye, something that I was doing as a poet – namely, exploring my own past, and my family's past, rooted in that specific social background. From this point of view, *Across a Roaring Hill* provided a critical counterpoint to an imaginative quest, both criss-crossing at the very vulnerable, crucial and even deadly intersection between 'region' (in my case, Protestant Belfast) and 'nation' (British or Irish).

Put simply, *Across a Roaring Hill* was, for me, a gesture to all those anonymous Protestants who saw literature as something alien to them and to what they considered as their 'way of life'. I wanted to establish, quite clearly, that some of Ireland's greatest writers in this century were, in fact, Protestant and that there was nothing inherently contradictory about such a state of affairs since it was the case: a reality to which they had rarely been exposed. In having this door opened to them, the real, brilliant complexity of literature might somehow be revealed, irrespective of categories of religion or definitions of place.

It would, in other words, be an ideal critical equation, paralleling what I found myself doing in poems: exploring the past, seeking clearly balanced moments of personal and historical tension and coincidences whereby one sees the influences, expectations and beliefs that govern one's own self image and, by implication, the community's out of which one came.

To what extent was there a 'Protestant imagination' or, more accurately, what creative valency ran between these two terms? This was the basic question which I felt needed some kind of answer. As a poet, I was trying to relate those writers in Ireland who meant something to me with the majority of other writers, not Irish, who were also personally significant. I was thinking of 'tradition' and trying to sort out the question of there being a coherent 'Protestant' literary tradition in which I could sound out my own experience in imaginative and cultural terms.

The answer is, I am convinced, that no such tradition exists in Ireland but, rather, as stated in the introduction to *Across A Roaring Hill*, that there is 'an eradicable consciousness of difference, of being defined in and against another culture' which makes, for instance, a 'direct descent in the Protestant line' still discernible, as in 'the evolution of forms and images from Yeats to MacNeice to Mahon'. Yet, like the term 'Anglo-Irish', the notion of a distinctly 'Protestant' literary tradition inevitably calls upon Yeats (or Burke or Swift) as 'the father' and, as W. J. McCormack points out in his *Ascendency and Tradition* (1985):

> Biological metaphors of this kind have an insidious effect in that they generate notions of a legitimising family tree which distinguishes the Anglo-Irish writer from a larger context instead of locating him in it.

My own personal and social experience resisted such notions of 'a legitimising family tree', seeing instead the disjointed, fragmentary nature of northern Protestantism. While this background offered people of my age the educational resources to move out into the wider community, it recoiled, for various specific historical factors, economic dependencies and religious susceptibilities, into a state of isolation – defensive and suspicious, constantly vigilant of possible betrayal and 'sell-out'. Belonging to such a tradition was, from the start, a very mixed blessing.

As Kafka remarked: 'my people, provided that I have one.' The 'return' to them is mined with anger and self-consciousness that can prove to be creatively crippling. Yet writers from such a Protestant background in Ireland are, ipso facto, more alert to the various undercurrents of meaning that one associates with terms like 'region' and 'nation', since they are never sure of their place in this system of things. They can take little for granted, except by a force of will or assumption. The community out of which they come is characterised by an obstinate silence in which trenchant dignity runs side-by-side with the triumphalism of the Orange Order or the noxious patronage of the Unionist Party, the twin ruling partners of the Protestant North. If these were 'my people', and they 'were sinking', as the Afrikaner novelist, André Brink, has written in *Mapmakers: Writing in a State of Siege* (1983), 'then it was their own fault, the inevitable retribution for what they themselves had done and allowed to be done'. Coming from such a background implicates the writer in a spider's web: the more one tries to draw away, the more entangled one becomes. This is how we described the situation in the introduction to *Across a Roaring Hill*:

> There is a heritage of guilt, repressed, formless and diffuse; and of tribal customs and binding beliefs which individuals – and writers – transgress at their peril: Calvinist cultures expel art from the city's gates, because they fear its power to penetrate communal neurosis – aggravated by such exclusion.

It is a fairly common experience of writers who seek to come to terms with a cultural inheritance, such as this, to have great difficulty coping with its religious bigotry and the prejudice that is itself an irrational protest against the world and evidence of an inability to understand it. What has happened in Northern Ireland is that, with such worldwide attention, the experience of ordinary people becomes contentious and can be easily converted into cliché and caricature – the processed suffering and recycled grievance, the everlasting 'victim', as much as the deluded superiority of insularity and bigotry. This places an added burden upon the writer and critic to ensure that what he or she writes is meticulously weighed against the political use to which it can be put.

Albert Camus' remark about the 'reserve' of the Breton writer Louis Guilloux, whom he greatly admired, is relevant here since Camus saw this artistic virtue as a way of preventing the writer from 'permitting the misery of others … to offer a picturesque subject for which the artist alone will not have to pay'. On another level, too, this reserve is an act of fidelity which establishes a self-critical distance rather than a falsely modest style of understatement. It relates not only to one's own politically grounded experience but also to the notion of 'tradition' itself: in my case, to a sanctified corpus of Irish literature in English that stretches from the 18th century to the present.

How could such a mythical continuum actually exist, given the profound economic, social, political and cultural changes that have happened in this country and, specifically, in that part of it in which I had grown up? It is a contradiction 'between tradition and its material' or, stated crudely, between the past and the present. To call upon W. J. McCormack's excellent *Ascendency and Tradition* again, this contradiction is 'a further statement of the disjunction between an Irish local literature and the European culture into which it cries out for reinsertion'.

In an atmosphere of great uncertainty and frustration, bitterness and hatred, when people turn to literature among other things as a means of overcoming religious and political divisions, it is difficult to take up that responsibility without, at the same time, running the risk of burdensome self-consciousness or, more importantly, of limiting, by definition, the way literature undermines every kind of division, from the 'regional' to the 'national'. On this Jacob's Ladder, which rung does one start on? Yet with various poetic voices of 'History' and 'Prophets of the People' being called for, to speak directly out of personal experience appears a mute, almost tame exercise in the flux of what is clearly a time of great tension and change. As the main character, Hans, says in *The Clown*, Heinrich Böll's novel about life in post-war Germany: '... the secret of the terror lay in the little things. To regret big things is child's play – political errors, adultery, murder, anti-Semitism – but who forgives, who understands the little things?' Sticking to a vigorous and exacting sense of what one knows and experiences assumes a kind of austere radicalism but, as so often happens with personal experience, when it becomes representative through the prism of literature, it can slide imperceptibly from being treated objectively towards being seen as picturesque and – in due course – imperilled by easy nostalgia.

The danger in all this, and one to which I trust *Across a Roaring Hill* was keenly alert, is suggested most cogently by Salman Rushdie in his essay 'Outside the Whale' (1984):

> ... there can be little doubt that in Britain today, the refurbishment of the Empire's tarnished image is under way. The continuing decline, the growing poverty, and the meanness of spirit of much of Thatcherite Britain, encourages many Britons to turn their eyes nostalgically to the lost hour of their precedence.

It is, of course, the Protestants of 'Northern Ireland', 'Ulster', 'the North' and the 'Six Counties', who are so visibly trapped in the 'lost hour of their precedence'. Given such meshing of literature, culture and politics, it is hardly surprising that, as Brian Friel remarked, 'everything is immediately perceived as political and the artist is burdened instantly with politicisation' (*Linen Hall Review*, Summer 1985). How to deal with politicisation is a question for the individual artist but what *kind* of politics is something we could all do with questioning. The trouble is that very often these two distinct, if not separate, issues get mixed up. For instance, in an insightful discussion of Field Day, Joe McMinn interprets the various critical responses to it as 'concealed political objections' to their 'dissemination of nationalist views of culture':

> Arguing for an apolitical analysis of Irish culture which will be sensible, moderate, rational, unemotional, dispassionate, is to take up

a political position without naming it. It is an extension of unionist political values into the cultural area.

*Fortnight*, September 1985

It is unclear precisely who is arguing for an apolitical analysis of Irish culture but of all the Heinz-varieties of unionism, I have not met with one that fits the bill here – sensible, moderate, detached and so on. The only political values that unionism has expressed are immoderation and an entrenched inability to be detached in *any* sense. (Nor, it should be said, is this the sole prerogative of unionism, as anyone will know who witnessed the moral debates in the Republic of Ireland on abortion and divorce.)

Confronting the historical impasse which a region called 'the North' is in, where unionism, whether it is liked or not, is the political voice of a substantial majority of the people who live there (and do not want, and will probably violently resist, belonging to a nation called 'Ireland'), there is an obvious imaginative and critical need to explore the experience of this people, their reasons for seeing life as they do and of placing this in the wider context (political, cultural and literary) of the whole country. In other words, to probe and possibly restore the shattered bonds of 'region' and 'nation' at an imaginative level which defines them both, bearing in mind the fact that the so-called question of 'the North' has no reality in isolation but is a part of, and a major critical influence upon, the 'Irish/British' question. It would be ironic, though, if such an aspiration was interpreted politically as propping up unionism.

Considering this relationship of 'region' to be an acknowledgement of diversity and difference within the ambit of 'nation', Seamus Deane, in his review of *Across a Roaring Hill*, wrote:

> Ireland must give its deference to difference and defer its 'unitary' ambitions. I find this interesting, but would like to have it identified more precisely. Is it a defence of Unionism cast in cultural terms? Or is it a plea for the recognition of a diversity which is in danger of being ignored?

*The Irish Times*, 14 September 1985

The answer is an emphatic Yes to the second question, as everyone engaged in these issues of 'region' and 'nation' must surely accept and support, else we lurch towards some covert or doctrinaire concept of authoritarian statehood. But against this reason, Enoch Powell in his *Times* review (15 August 1985) saw *Across a Roaring Hill* as one in a line of work 'much petted and encouraged by those, in Great Britain and elsewhere, who want to bully the Northern Ireland electorate out of their settled conviction to remain within the United Kingdom'. Rather than being a putative defence of unionism, the book is seen as attacking it. Furthermore, Declan Kiberd in *Fortnight* (November 1985) saw Alliance Party liberal do-gooders nicking around between the book's covers.

One can see at this stage where the burden of politicisation, of which Brian Friel speaks, slides into gyres of rhetoric. The complex ways that human feeling is meshed with cultural affiliation evaporate and the actual manipulators of political identity (who, after all, control and embody power) get off the hook. What is more, it treats the experience of others (northern Protestants, in this instance) to a further illustration of the kind of fashionable disdain they have come to expect and denies that very diversity in Irish life which demands recognition, if the relationship between 'region' and 'nation' is ever going to be an unbloody one. To define and elucidate these different kinds of experience and ideas is, I would have thought, an essential obligation if we are ever going to understand adequately the state Ireland is in, never mind realising the one that many of us hope it will become. This is one definite place where the writer has an important role to play, as André Brink suggests, 'of fighting to assert the most positive and creative aspects of his heritage'. And we should not forget all those who, over the years, to quote Christopher Hitchens, have challenged 'their own tribes with criticism, opposition and argument from within' (*Prepared for the Worst*, 1990). It is important to add here that this imaginative struggle is, as Brink says, also often against those who 'can afford to clash with authority because they are basically protected by it'.

If there is, as I believe there to be, a world of difference between the experience of Protestant families in the North, their feelings, fears, hopes and ambitions (the stuff one hears so much pious talk about in the Republic) and the political use made of them, then the crucial discrimination must be made and maintained between the two sets of experiences and the various economic, social and cultural bonds that keep them bound together.

Should this effort at understanding be daubed 'Unionist', we will have missed another chance of exposing the invidious forms of falsehood and violence which oppress people on the small island of Ireland; and have done so because of fashionable intellectual posturing, not out of real political commitment and work. For it is an effort of knowing the past which requires us, as Peter Gay well knew on the truly horrendous scale of his native Germany, to 'mobilize historical understanding and to make discriminations [which do] not mean to deny or to prettify what has happened' (*Freud, Jews and Other Germans*, 1978).

*Across a Roaring Hill* was just a small part of the process whereby prevailing mythologies and the ways they are, in turn, transformed into literary art, are opened up and brought into the light of day. It is a first step: exploratory and, within its limits, diverse and speculative. As this process comes under an imaginatively sustained criticism, everything is up for grabs; not just a monolithic 'Irish' literary tradition, but the very notion of 'tradition' itself, the language used to discuss these things and our working through the inherited ways of seeing them both. This is the truly radical challenge that the present offers; not painting ourselves back into a corner of the killing floor which so often seems to be the case in Ireland.

The relationship between a 'Protestant' or 'Catholic', 'nationalist' or 'unionist' experience is only one (if presently dominant) cultural and political distinction. Like all labels, they bear the marks of prejudice from which few are free. One has to take into account, however, entire tracks of historical and contemporary experience that are of very real significance in Ireland today – 'loyalty' and the question of 'belonging', such as that considered in Thomas Kilroy's play *Double Cross*, or the force field of community and the individual's own complicated place within it which John McGahern has explored in *High Ground* – to say nothing about the explosion of women's writing in Ireland in recent times.

These are issues that come readily to my own mind since I have an abiding interest in them as a writer, but they underpin the present and are bound to have serious implications for the kind of literature (and politics) that many want to see taking over from the current conventions and official dogmas. I think this is the point behind Seamus Deane's close reading of *Across a Roaring Hill* when, in singling out Bridget O'Toole's essay on Jennifer Johnston, Elizabeth Bowen and Molly Keane, he writes:

> ... a sentence from Elizabeth Bowen ... might have been this volume's epigraph and ... has its application, economic and cultural, for Protestants and Catholics: 'We have everything to dread from the dispossessed'. It is in dispossession that the hurt, Protestant and Catholic, lies.

Material deprivation and cultural dispossession are indeed fundamental 'themes', since they are the common inheritance of so many Irish men and women. It would be a shame if this fact was lost sight of and turned, on the lathe of dogma, into an obligatory truth from which those who actually live it out can find no real imaginative release or critical yet sympathetic distance. As Terence Brown eloquently put it in his Field Day pamphlet, *The Whole Protestant Community: The Making of an Historical Myth*:

> A people who have known resistance as well as dissent, rebellion, dispute, religious enthusiasm in the midst of rural and urban deprivation, have an interesting story to tell themselves – one of essential homelessness, dependency, anxiety, obdurate fantasising, sacrifices in the name of liberty, villainous political opportunism, moments of idealistic aspiration. And in the telling of it they may come to realise at last where they are most at home and with whom they share that home.

The colloquial 'Tell us a story' goes far beyond a child's need for reassurance; it opens out the ground of imaginative possibility as well. What we are seeing in Ireland today is a clash between the traditional ways of perceiving these possibilities and the need to bypass the politics which stunts them. The writer is caught – appropriately enough – in the middle.

[1986]

# FALSE FACES

There is little doubt that a profound, if fragmented, conflict of interest is taking place throughout Ireland today, on both political and economic levels. It does seem, however, that little creative thought has been directed its way. Instead an 'identity crisis' predominates. Filtered through the sieve of literature, this 'crisis' has removed the need to address the economic, political and religious power-structures which govern most of our lives on both sides of the border. What is also noticeable is the extent to which we seem to be minesweeping Irish literature for markers of weakness and woe: a mutilated tongue, a broken culture – charges that interpret our pain and anger but make a privileged outrage of the history rather than the experience of life in Ireland today. This seems only to perpetuate those categories of victimised/oppressed/colonised from which we seek to liberate ourselves. There is a domino effect involved.

Irish Literature has in the past used and stressed (by focusing upon, if nothing else) issues like the uncertain, fraught possession of the English language, both as historical fact and as imaginative counterpart. These have been potently fused in Irish culture, mirroring each other. But in the process, critics have, in their turn, concentrated upon the thematic confluence distinct from its contingent being as art. They have confused life with art, art with history and the result has been self-perpetuating: fashionable ideas and images have turned into clichés the still authentic symbols of Irish experience. This does not, however, challenge the way we are or perceive ourselves to be, while the economic and political status quo is clearly untroubled by such discussion. It may well be time, in other words, to start all over again.

In *Heroic Styles: The Tradition of an Idea* (reprinted in *Ireland's Field Day*, 1985), Seamus Deane seems to be saying approximately the same thing through his scrutiny of what lies behind many of our cultural assumptions, specifically as they relate to and out of the North:

> The communities have become stereotyped into their roles of oppressor and victim to such an extent that the notion of a Protestant or a Catholic sensibility is now assumed to be a fact of nature rather than a product of these very special and ferocious conditions.

The Field Day pamphlets are designed to relate 'these very special and ferocious conditions' theoretically to a new approach, to what has been called 'The Fifth Province' and defined as 'an equivalent centre from which the four broken and fragmented pieces of contemporary Ireland might be seen in fact coherent.'

The idea is invigorating, yet the response to it has varied from the mute to the hostile. In her *Irish Times* review of Seamus Heaney's *An Open Letter*, Eavan Boland, seeming both cautious and uncertain about the Fifth Province and what it stood for, was specific on one point:

> A new Ulster nationalism is not my idea of what Irish poetry needs, but I would be quite willing to lay aside this prejudice if the new nationalism contained all the voices, all the fragments, all the dualities and ambiguities of reference; but it doesn't. Judging by the ... pamphlets here in front of me, this is green nationalism and divided culture. 'Whatever we mean by the Irish situation,' writes Derek Mahon, 'the shipyards of Belfast are no less a part of it than a country town in the Gaeltacht.' Would that this were true; or, at least, would that it were real.

Seamus Deane is clearly conscious of this absent voice when he talks about breaking down stereotypes:

> ... by making people have the confidence that each of us has a culture that's not going to disappear if it comes in contact with the other. But it's a kind of confidence severely lacking in Unionists, which is why they're so neurotically defensive. That's the problem with Field Day. It's no good just performing our plays and selling pamphlets to people we know. There's no point in continuing unless we can get through to Unionists.

It is not only the unionists who are 'neurotically defensive' and lacking in 'confidence' but there is a much more important point to be made here. It is unclear where the Fifth Province bears upon this absent voice and also whether there is, in realisable terms, a culture that can be defined as 'Protestant' and unionist. It depends, of course, upon how one defines culture but, taking that term in its widest sense, it is fair to say that the Protestant/unionist sense of self derives its meaning (and is 'neurotically defensive' for this very reason) from the fact of its being undefined, imaginatively and historically. The famed inarticulateness, the Ulster that says No!, is, after all, a perfectly legitimate right to silence. In a way, the Protestant/unionist culture has no image of itself and consequently accepts those stereotypes which have been created for political purposes, be that within Northern Ireland or from London or Dublin. Stereotypes which are believed in. An important step would therefore be to begin a process of critical definition if only to reveal the illegitimacy of those terms of reference and to establish new, imaginative ones. Yet, in dealing with *Anglo-Irish Attitudes* Declan Kiberd addresses himself variously to 'British liberals', 'British writers' and 'English liberals', the very dependency which the Fifth Province justly challenges. As he does elsewhere in his pamphlet when he criticises those, such as F.S.L. Lyons, who have received 'praises and prizes' from the English. However, it 'is certainly time', writes Kiberd

> ... that British intellectuals applied themselves to a critical analysis of unionism, what it represents, and what it is doing to Britain as a whole.

'British writers' must '... apply themselves to the study of Ulster Unionism'; English intellectuals have also virtually excluded 'any informed assessment of the deeper meanings of Ulster Unionism'.

I have suggested elsewhere that writers and critics in Ireland should consider the 'deeper meanings', not simply of Ulster unionism, but the entirety of 'Protestant' experience in the North and the common ground northerners share, irrespective of religion, as northeners. To ask the English to do so seems a fairly reasonable request (and perhaps witness to a new genre: an Anglo-Northern-Irish literature, a three-headed hybrid), although hardly in keeping with the Fifth Province. But if, as Declan Kiberd suggests, 'in modern Ulster men's emotions have been ruled not so much by culture as by cash', then the solution will lie in that direction and the 'full understanding of the situation in Ireland today' resolved on that score, whatever about the current intellectual fuss.

But the unverifiability of so much talk about 'identity' springs from a severance from common experience and its established terms of negative feeling being sympathetically and imaginatively absorbed – hatred, anger, insecurity, bigotry and fear. These forms are fed by particularly virulent forms of supremacy which are themselves reliant upon political and social power-structures throughout the entire country. Only in the North have these become a matter of life and death and they pervade every area of contention. It is these terms and their institutionalised structures which will have to be transformed, from the inside, while the dependencies they ritualise will have to be understood and rewritten, before the simple human and ideological barriers to unity are breached in a meaningful and lasting way.

One notes an implicit interpretation of history as if it were a machine (or monster) which, partially of its own making, but mainly of English making, conscribes 'the Irish' to a world of thought detached from independent action (or creation). 'History' is populated by brutalised marionettes who continue to dominate the way we think and imagine we feel. But the creative and critical dislocation which takes place as a result of the situation does not illuminate the emotional and subjective bonds that keep both sides in the northern community locked in what has been described by Thomas Kilroy as 'a struggle for the irretrievable'. It is this struggle which has most often been dealt with at the level of self-fulfilling ideas; otherwise, as Richard Kearney remarks in *Myth and Motherland*, it is feared 'we capitulate to the mindless conformism of fact'. But facts are not mindless and they dominate only when we perceive them abstractly; cascading into vicious cycles, they are seen as unfit for our solving preconceptions. Up close, fixed in the imagination and historical reason, they have all the energy of life, its power-struggles and their moral and political consequences.

History is not to blame but people, and the way the two have drifted apart into exclusive orthodoxies. That is the problem: the human complexity. But when ideas get caught up with only themselves and loosen their moorings in personal experience and historical reality, despite the intention of their being addressed to present social and political conditions, then that critical dialectic has been broken and it is the intellectual process which fossilises, not the world these ideas are intended to change.

There is a conviction which influences much of the discussion about 'Identity' that a fundamental unity actually underlies Irish culture if only the people could (or would) see it. Whatever about the political manipulation of this ideal and the conflicting forms it takes, it must be time for writers and critics to explore all the shades of its creative viability.

In saying this I am not suggesting as some may, imitating Johnson's anti-Berkelyan boot against the boulder, that on the rock of one million Protestants thy dreams will perish. Such attitudes betray intolerance and a fear of change. Rather I am saying that a radical shift of attention is needed. For, in a way, the Protestants of the North of Ireland are peripheral since the critical focus of definition does not involve them. They are, and have always been, a belligerent and beleaguered third party, reacting to the various realignments that have taken place between the dominant two of 'Ireland' and 'England', so that no matter what 'solution' is arrived at, they will, more than likely, remain outside it, against the current. They are, though, symbols of a much deeper malaise in the whole country since it no longer has (if it ever had) a cultural unity. By their very existence, along with so much else of contemporary and historical experience which is either left out of the picture or modishly caricatured, they threaten such ideals. As a result, they are portrayed as dull, dour, pragmatic – the usual epithets that say about as much on 'northern Protestants' as similar glosses say about the Republic.

Some take glum satisfaction in this situation; others see northern Protestant intransigence as one example of those historical facts and cultural conditions which need imaginative exploration, not exploitation. This exploitation has led to the oppressive edifice of the Northern Irish state while permitting the deceit of nationalism (and superficial reactions against it) to make fools or victims of us all.

There is no prescriptive answer here. For the response of the individual imagination is born of a need to get through as best it can to whomever cares to listen. The mediating role of the print and broadcasting world is crucial here. For example, take *The Irish Reporter*, an important left-of-centre journal, published in Dublin. In a recent issue, there are photographs of Protestants at play. In one of them a woman, doing a knees-up, shows off her knickers; in the background an Orangeband. Side on, the title declares THE PROTESTANTS. The facing page carries a statement from Sinn Féin on their struggle to improve the quality of life of Irish people. There are other articles dealing with post-colonialism but, stuck there in the back pages is that unrepentant Protestant woman, having a good time.

Subtextually, she is unredeemable in terms of visual messages. The photograph is a covert sign of an intellectual distaste; for this is no folk session – not in the acceptable sense of either word. This is beyond the pale of cultural and political credibility. Like her people, she is 'incorrect', as the Twelfth bonfire in Tiger's Bay. But change the context to an Irish emigrant centre in Manchester and one can imagine the justifiable anger at this anti-feminist and racist exploitation.

Over recent years, intellectual and cultural attitudes have hardened towards northern Protestants and, particularly, to those who consider the union with Britain to be a personal and emotional lifeline separate from the perceived introversions and hypocrisies of the Catholic country to the south and west.

This hardening or dismissiveness is a reflection of a general switch-off in the Republic to the North itself. The place seems stuck in a groove few in the Republic have much private time for – the old historical business of fighting the Brits has not, as Sinn Féin knows, cut too much parliamentary ice in the 26 counties.

Similarly, the once assumed dominance of northern writing – or writers from the North – has meant that southern writers – or writers based in the south – have become much less sensitive to what goes on North of the border. Attitudes vary between truculence, indifference to fed-up-ness about what precisely a writer's attitude should be to the events in the North and to the nature of the achievement of the writing that has come from writers born there. The reaction to the *Field Day Anthology* was in part a reaction against the northern-ness of its declared political and cultural concerns, primarily, with national identity.

Sensibilities were already geared to attack Field Day and the protracted gestation of its anthological statement on Irish writing. Field Day had, by the end of the 1980s, started to look a little out of step with cultural and political issues in the Republic – questions about private morality and public corruption, the scandals of emigration and commercial greed – and, as we all now know, the fundamental sea-change that took place in the self-perception of women in Irish society.

Yet it is a curious feature of the anthology itself that it shares a 'pan-Irish' uncertainty when addressing the work, within its own political ambit, of writers from the northern Protestant background. It is a feature which Damian Smyth jumped on in his condemnation of what he saw as the monolithic dogmatism of Field Day's nationalism:

> What cannot be totalised is left out, and the intellectual ethnic-cleansing which sees the absence of the Rhyming Weavers is only slightly less crude in the treatment of the user-friendly Prods of the nationalist discourse.
>
> *Fortnight*, September 1992

Whether or not the absence of the *Rhyming Weavers* constitutes a capital offence artistically is open to question. On historical grounds the omission is regrettable. The failure to select a just sample of women's writing is, however, inexcusable. As for the 'user-friendly Prods', it is instructive to see the manner in which two of them are described in the anthology.

It has to be said that the headnotes vary from the almost apocalyptic eagerness with which John Montague is cast 'unashamedly in the bardic role of spokesman for the tribe', to the subdued etiquette of Michael Longley's 'self-effacing courtesy, his dry good humour'. Longley is, however, inexplicably defined in terms of the 'semi-detached suburban muse of Philip Larkin and ... British post-modernism, as is manifest in his homage to L. S. Lowry'. There is in this summary absolutely no accounting for the surreal, the love lyrics, the bizarre and the classical in Longley, all of which coalesce to make a poetry constitutionally different from the despairing symbolism of Philip Larkin.

Longley is also paired with Mahon in a siamese-twinning of cultural aspiration whereby both poets are taken to represent 'a strand of Ulster that identifies itself as British and asserts its rights to the English lyric'.

Mahon is 'the most underrated Irish poet of the century' – underrated by whom? – and the ontological frame of being 'a post-holocaust poet' is hedged in the following terms as one who 'may yet prove to be the most durable talent of his generation. He writes not just of, but for, posterities'.

These uncertainties suggest the wide intellectual instability when it comes to addressing the cultural and literary issues of northern Protestantism. Longley is conscripted to history as an Irish Larkin while Mahon exists in a futuristic critical limbo.

The significance of this unease plays across the cultural and political life of Ireland. It moderates from good-humoured banter and wit, perplexity and arrogance to bewilderment and contempt with an average in sorrow, bemusement and superiority complexes all round.

'Protestants' are considered 'unionists' (or, more fashionably, 'neo-unionists') unless they publicly declare to the contrary and seek asylum in 'Irish Literature'. Failure to do so unsettles the kind of cultural agendas that the media, publishing and academic worlds rely upon, both in Ireland and abroad.

In an interview in *The Irish Times* on the occasion of being awarded the Whitbread Prize for his collection *Gorse Fires*, Michael Longley remarked on the selection from his work in the Field Day anthology:

> I object to being embalmed wearing a false face, a mask. I feel diminished and travestied. I had thought of asking to be withdrawn from subsequent editions, but it seemed self-important.
>
> *The Irish Times*, 11 January 1992

The sense of not having the freedom to be one's self (to be considered on one's own imaginative ground, so to speak) but inhibited instead by cultural priorities not of one's own making, leads to all sorts of negations and misrepresentations. How could it be, though, that an anthology of this magnitude, such an extraordinary achievement in so very many ways, should end up with calls for it to be pulped and other suggestions of withdrawal?

From the convicted 'terrorist' in a prison in the south of Ireland reciting his poems about 'Ireland' that sound little different from the rhetoric of the 19th-century Young Irelanders, to the designer caricatures surrounding the term 'northern Protestant', it is tempting to see all writing from Ireland as forever folkloric, underpinned by regional or national loyalties and political designs. This is folly, to quote the critic Patrick Wright, because it toys with the idea that politics can be conjured out of cultural roots at will. Should this be where we are all heading, poetry had better look to its laurels.

[1985–1993]

# LIVING IN OUR OWN TIME:
## Yeats and Power

In his introduction to *Yeats* (1971) in the Fontana Modern Masters series, Denis Donoghue described Yeats' attitude to society in the following terms:

> ... his mind turns unwillingly to detail, unless the detail is a nuance of feeling. He admired notable people, but his respect for ordinary people as constituting a particular society and living a certain life at a certain time was extremely weak; when he looked beyond the chosen few he saw a fictive race rather than a finite society.

I am not sure that this is absolutely true since Yeats used the chosen few friends and companions as bridges into the wider world, a public world, and he operated there with enthusiasm and dedication; but the gesture Donoghue is describing seems representative in another way. For in our 'post Yeatsian' Ireland we still think of 'the Irish' as a fictive race, while 'a finite society' is quite clearly not a priority, and this holds true whether we are talking about the North or the south of Ireland. Somehow or other, society, civic space, has evaporated into thin air, along with the assumed rights and responsibilities of our being, quite simply, citizens. This evasion, for such it is, has all kinds of implications for literature and literary criticism. It means, for instance, that the role of the writer in Irish society is intimately bound up with compensating rather than with questioning. In place of a social world, in which each citizen performs certain basic obligations and receives, in return, certain freedoms, our literary culture (in the main) shoulders this responsibility and becomes a chronicle of failure.

Failed obligations, inadequate freedoms – with the net result that Irish novels, poems, plays and criticism often deal with what is not the case rather than with what is. The writer's inheritance is to negotiate with the supposed ideal world, and the fall from such grace; the finite society exists elsewhere, like poor old England.

The reasons for this slippage are much too complicated to go into here but one cannot help noticing the extent to which Irish literature, and the critical reception it receives, is haunted by a greater past while the present is treated with disdain. Ireland *now* has to be bad news (or dressed up as a yuppie paradise!); the future or the past is infinitely better.

The political draft of this influence is plain to everyone. We do not have to look at the exact human effects of this or that political act because, basically, politics does not really happen in Ireland. What we have are messianic strategies, earthed in historical overviews and sacred landscapes or the job lottery of international 'diplomacy'. Talk to anyone under the age of forty, and hear for yourself the chief reason for the exodus from the country; read the poetry and prose that is churned out week after week for publication in the few magazines and newspapers that bother to offer a decent platform for Irish writers at home. The message is quite emphatic: in spite of all the grand talk, 'Ireland' is breaking down. What will take its place is, of course, the big question.

Strangely, Denis Donoghue does not really give this much thought. On the very first page of *We Irish: Essays on Irish Literature and Society* (1986), he introduces the selection of essays and reviews with an unusual reservation:

> There seemed little merit bringing forward an essay on Long Kesh and the Hunger-Strikes, which appeared in *The New York Review of Books* in October 1981; the issues raised by that event were immediate and intense, but it would be tendentious to bring them up again.

Just because something appears at one time 'immediate and intense' does not debar it from lasting significance. But the Hunger Strikes as 'tendentious'? The ghastly point about the Hunger Strikes must surely be, as Sean O'Faoláin pointed out in his *London Review of Books* article at the same time, that they were (are?) part of an Irish belief in sacrifice, and that sacrifice is seen not as a denial of political possibility but as its consummation. This denotes a remarkable relation to the world.

It only requires the briefest of looks at Irish drama to see how one of our literary traditions first inspired this belief (Yeats) and then progressively tried to disengage from it (O'Casey, Denis Johnston, Behan). It is precisely around an issue like the Hunger Strikes that the cultural, spiritual and political assumptions surface and bring in their wake the dark secretive nuances of feeling that Yeats understood so much better than many a contemporary commentator. And after him too, a poet such as Padraic Fiacc has constantly turned to that desperate, tragic strain in Irish experience. Yet Fiacc is not mentioned in Donoghue's *The Literature of Trouble* as a poet, only as editor of the anthology *The Wearing of the Black* (1974).

When he is on firmer ground, such as 'The European Joyce' or the fine *Sewanee Review* piece, 'Together', Donoghue's intellectual arguments are precise and invigorating. It is disarming though, in this battery of cross reference and perceptive readings, to come across another tilt in the direction of Stephen Dedalus' scene with the Dean of Studies and Seamus Heaney's refashioning of this 'acquired speech' for his own purposes in *Station Island*. Donoghue is less than convinced, it has to be said, but one would have preferred a clearer critical conclusion to the title essay, 'We Irish', than the somewhat bemused (and subtextually bored?) remark: 'It is probably wise for some poets to brood as little as possible upon their being Irish and to let the constituents of their poetry settle down without fuss'. A touch disingenuous given the title, 'We Irish'?

Where Donoghue brings a slight sense of elevated dismay to his topics, Edna Longley comes out fighting in *From Cathleen to Anorexia* (1990), knowing the ropes (and who made them) like the back of her hand. Ms Longley has precious few illusions left about 'a fictive race'. She hates the sight of such blather and is understandably impatient, to the point of intolerance, with any writer who breathes life into the bloody old beast. Ms Longley is for the finitude of society and the transcendence of art but where they intersect is, shall we say, a moot point?

What I find most convincing about her pamphlet is that there are no holds barred, although I wonder if the literary discrimination occasionally slips in the interests of establishing a canonical hit-list, from Field Day via John Hume to the taking to task of Eavan Boland for her LIP pamphlet, *A Kind of Scar: The Woman Poet in a National Tradition* (1989). Without going into the ins-and-outs of the question, it strikes me that Boland does question the 'National Tradition' as much as the male-dominated literary culture. She sees nationalism, after all, as 'a necessary hallucination within Joyce's nightmare of history', but obviously her disengagement is not sufficient for Ms. Longley's purposes:

> ... because she [Boland] does not blame Nationalism her alliterative muse turns out to be the twin sister of Dark Rosaleen: 'the truths of womanhood and the defeats of a nation: an improbable intersection?'

The question is Boland's but Longley's rejection of the tentative answer is unconditional:

> Boland's new muse ... looks remarkably like the Sean Bhean Bhoct ... By not questioning the nation, Boland recycles the literary clichés from which she desires to escape.

But questioning the nation might not lead anywhere either, so far as literature goes. As Ms. Longley points out elsewhere, Virgin-Ireland as Proud or Sorrowful Widow, Defiant Daughter or Long-Suffering Mother are the kinds of images many Irish and British activist writers were brought up on. Whereas a question here or there about contemporary Irish experience (in the Republic, for instance) might lead to work of a socially revealing nature, particularly from the viewpoint of women writing, there is absolutely no guarantee that the artistic virtue of such writing exceeds what was once described as hasty writing about the North's 'Troubles'. The agenda has moved on, that is all, but how has the poetry, prose or drama been interpreted if not as just one more vehicle for voicing dissent from, or a need for, the 'fictive race'? Could it not well be that imaginative inspiration and vitality lie somewhere else altogether?

The burden of market values is being put formidably upon literature while the metaphorical question remains, to quote from Richard Murphy's *The Battle of Aughrim*: 'To whom will the land belong/This time tomorrow night?' That issue of authority and a negotiated settlement of power can be sublimated into as many texts as there are political prisoners, but only an honest, responsible and just constitutional structure can resolve it. From then on people will make (or not make) the necessary adjustments, as was done in the Free State during its turbulent birth, and in every other European country, not to forget the struggle for civil rights in the US, bloody débâcle as that was.

In an instructive sense, we can trace this prefigurement in the poetry of Richard Murphy. In his *New Selected Poems* (1989) the development is from a poet preoccupied with the history of his family and its role in Irish life to the metaphorical home his poetry can build for himself, such as the sonnet sequence, 'The Price of Stone'.

Ironically, Murphy has been shunted aside in much of 'the Debate' so far. He does not feature, for instance, in Donoghue's *Yeats, Ancestral Houses, and Anglo-Ireland* and one would have thought Ms Longley might have quoted his poem 'Amazement' as an apt illustration alongside the Irish ballad of Muldoon's 'Aisling'.

It may be that Murphy's knowledge of Irish life alludes paradoxically to a respect for ordinary people, for the particularity of their society and that this manner, which amounts to the creation of an entire world in his poetry, has become unintelligible to contemporary ideological schemes. This would be a great pity because Murphy has bridged various kinds of cultural divides himself – between England and Ireland; the rich erotic world of Sri Lanka in *The Mirror Wall* (1989) to the imperial decay of Ceylon; the outcast in society and the possibility of freedom within a sexually repressed culture such as Ireland's where the deadly stasis of history is no longer capable of sustaining or inspiring the majority of its people. His palpable concern for language and the skills of his verse-making are also an ever-present indictment of what so often passes for poetry in Ireland. If we are to make ourselves into a new image it might be no harm to remember that we have to do it through a language of union:

Although we have no home in the time that's come,
Coming together we live in our own time.

[1990]

# JUST IMAGES: On Regionalism

In *The Dark Sun*, his book on Lawrence, Graham Hough remarked:

> The contrast between the provincial childhood and the cosmopolitan later life has been overplayed. Childhood is always provincial, and its horizon always restricted ... [a] rather hoity-toity concept of culture has been used to show that Lawrence had a hole-and-corner upbringing, and remained therefore an inspired barbarian, ignorant of the grand calm expanses of properly certified European civilisation. But the only people who ever inhabit this kind of civilisation are cultivated Americans, like Henry James or Mr. Eliot; Europeans live in Nottingham or Nancy, Paris or Piacenza, Frankfurt or Fenny Stratford, and the actual life of any of these places has always seemed a poor and disappointing affair to visitors from the platonic New England heights.

Not bad for 1956 (thus *Mr.* Eliot) but Hough's point is equally damning when we think of the time and energy spent in Ireland riddling out Patrick Kavanagh's distinction between parochialism (a certain good) and provincialism (a definite no-no). Screeds have been filled, too, on the topic of cosmopolitanism in Irish literature as against the rootedness of Irish life. Indeed, the perceived tension between the two has become a theme of much contemporary writing in English: Heaney, Walcott, Harrison, Murray ... inspired barbarians all.

As Hough says, we all come from somewhere; where we go to is another day's work. Somehow, in Ireland, there is a kind of sanctity about this original relationship: an inherited piety, defying scrutiny, that bobs around in an ether of accent, nudges and winks, aspiration and ambition. We all know what is meant even as little change is ever made of home through imaginative and cultural interpretations.

Where one is from in Ireland, all that mire of anecdotage which so often conceals an old-fashioned hunger for power, prestige and authority, defines 'the self' before one can literally open one's mouth. Of recent times, the politics of place has taken over the place of politics in our lives. This is a shame. In a way, regionalism is some kind of answer.

When I think of regionalism, though, I think of the greatest provincial traditions in literature and the visual arts in France, or the example of a writer like Franz Kafka who engaged at such a deep imaginative level with his own religious and linguistic background in Prague. In Ireland, regionalism seems to mean something else entirely: Dáil Connacht in the late '60s and '70s, or a group of fugitives seeking political time-out, a cultural breathing-space in the '80s. Or it assumes the double-take of fidelity, using the culture one has come from as an imaginative and linguistic crutch before learning to walk, metaphorically speaking, in the big bad world. The vernacular as empire-breaker can so easily be turned inside out, especially by a culture, such as England's or Ireland's, which lacks powerful European-style provincial traditions in art and literature. So what regionalism will mean in and to the '90s is anyone's guess.

Honour, reserve, distance, understanding, anger, respect: these are all words that come to mind when one thinks about place. Region and regionalism are, instead, awkward substitutes designed to take the heat out but give back little in return, other than the digital glow of an agenda, with its key words (Identity and so forth) and expected social practices: dour northerners, slick Dublinmen, dreamy westerners and the like.

For what it's worth, I come from no region called 'Northern Ireland', 'Ulster' or the 'Six Counties'. I come from Belfast, born and bred on the northside, schooled on the east, and in these particular districts, with known avenues and persistent views, attitudes and assumptions, my own speech was formed. Everything is conducted in and through that medium. What one does with such an inheritance calls upon chance, choice and the luck of the Muses. It is a recalcitrant, disturbed and unsettling past in the main and I envy the way many Irish writers interpret 'home' as a substitute literary reality of consoling artifice. So art makes up for the impoverished present and past without which there would be no poem or play in the first place. One wonders where self-irony has gone to and the necessary sense of proportion when a comparison is made between Irish history and mainland Europe of the post-1914 era.

## II

When Seamus Heaney writes about Kavanagh and MacNeice in *The Government of the Tongue*, he sees in the latter's *Collected Poems* 'the window-pane of literature ... a mind-stuff [that] existed in a cultural setting which was at one remove from me and what I came from'. While fingering 'their security in the big world of history and poetry that happened out there', one senses a value-laden region of the mind taking political shape in Heaney. Whether Kavanagh 'wanted it or not, his achievement was inevitably co-opted, North and south, into the general current of feeling which flowed from and sustained ideas of national identity, cultural otherness from Britain and the dream of a literature with a manner and a matter resistant to the central Englishness of the dominant tradition'.

Thus the case for the prosecution, circa 1961. Britain and Englishness come from somewhere else though (i.e. 1986), and they would have meant next to nothing to the likes of us in the '50s and '60s, who never understood either place or quality, and, to be frank, still don't.

When Edna Longley calls the North 'a cultural corridor' (*From Cathleen to Anorexia*, 1990), regionalism is being brought into play. For Heaney's 'national identity, cultural otherness' read 'a zone where Ireland and Britain permeate one another'. The suggestion of fluidity here (permeate) is appealing, but the notion of more boundaries (corridor) in some indistinct way poses more problems that it can hope to solve. After all, corridors must *lead* somewhere and what might be working in a poem (the translation of influences) is a totally different story when it comes to politics and the struggle for power.

It could well be that my own upbringing, in eluding real cultural definition, took too much for granted; that what looked like ease was really anxiety: the thought which has crossed so many minds throughout these islands about what one actually belongs to – a state, a nation, a place, an idea, an illusion, or just images?

Understanding where one has come from evokes a physical place but also a temporal order; the business of history, and how often the call is made for 'us' to master it. This is one of the strategies of regionalism but, lacking a political space which will make opinions significant and actions effective, one wonders what can come of all this talk.

In her excellent collection of essays, *Men in Dark Times* (1968) Hannah Arendt, who knew about exile and oppression, wrote:

> Insofar as any 'mastering' of the past is possible it consists in relating what has happened; but such narration, too, which shapes history, solves no problems and assuages no suffering; it does not master anything once and for all. Rather, as long as the meaning of the events remains alive ... 'mastering the past' can take the form of ever-recurrent narration. The poet in a very general sense and the historian in a very special sense have the task of setting this process of narration in motion and of involving us in it.

It does not matter what word you give this process so long as it happens. Where the poet fits in is, more than likely, just to make poems and let them speak for themselves; the principal loyalty which has everything to do with a private sense of a place and its people.

[1992]

# CARLETON'S ADDRESS

In Northern Ireland people are known by their address – where you are from is a key to who and what you are. That is the historical reality of address. There is another meaning, though – of addressing people, speaking to them. This meaning has a somewhat rhetorical flourish to it that can degenerate into polemical or ideological bilge. From individual fate to the collective discourse within which every writer features, there are many pitfalls, delusions, traps, and, as with circus mirrors, self-distortions. Some of these energies and perceptions are present in the writing of the nineteenth century, Irish novelist, William Carleton.

In the preface to his novel *The Tithe Proctor* (1849) William Carleton writes:

> I endeavour to paint Ireland sometimes as she was but always as she is, in order that she may see many of those debasing circumstances which prevent her from being what she ought to be.

Carleton's insistence that his work is derived from actual fact ('always as she is') implies the moral rectitude of those conclusions which he may draw ('that she may see many of those debasing circumstances which prevent her from being what she ought to be'). His desire to 'bear witness' recalls Joyce's Stephen Dedalus, almost a century after him:

> ... I shall go to encounter for the millionth time the reality of experience and to forge in the smithy of my soul the uncreated conscience of my race.

Through the drafts of *Stephen Hero* and *A Portrait*, Joyce refined his novel until it penetrated to the essence of his central character's development and revealed this development in each of its stages – infancy, childhood, adolescence and manhood. The control and poise of *A Portrait* flows from Joyce's mastery of the artistic resources available to him and his own unique extension of these resources. He was a meticulous craftsman who, in shaping his work, was guided by the principle inherent in that rhetorical phrase – to forge the conscience of the Irish race. The ironic undertones of 'forge' – to shape, to advance but also to counterfeit, anticipates the multi-level meanings of *Ulysses*. In Carleton 'to forge' was a direct, moral duty.

Follow Joyce through *A Portrait, Ulysses,* and *Finnegans Wake,* and what we see is the subtle progressive deepening of his ideas – as matters concerned with artistic expression and the sufficiency of language. No such development occurs in Carleton's work. While Joyce extended and deepened the significance of his work, creating wider and more intricate patterns of expression, Carleton returned constantly to a basic literary model. Some critics account for this lack of artistic development by describing Carleton as an 'instinctive writer' who found the novel form alien. (Anthony Cronin, 'The Dark Side of Carleton', *The Irish Times*, 5 April 1974). In this view Carleton is seen as a writer of whom, in drawing his inspiration from the work of folk-belief and custom, we should not expect the same degree of artistic self-consciousness that we find in an artist like Joyce. This view glosses over several important points.

The endeavour to 'bear witness', to record the plight and condition of the Irish peasants, 'The People', was primary in Carleton. Yet this desire could be realised only if it was rooted in a deepening creative awareness of the problems inherent in such an attempt. Any one of Carleton's novels may achieve this, but the fact that he was unable to deepen his range throughout the corpus of his work demonstrates the limitations of his talent. It also illustrates the inadequacy of looking upon Carleton as an 'instinctive writer' and of leaving it at that. After all, Carleton saw himself as a novelist.

He did come in contact with the native story-teller or seanchaí. His autobiography affectionately recalls the image of his father, who, if not a professional seanchaí, possessed the story-teller's skill in reciting and animating story and song. The seanchaí told tales by the fireside, tales the origins of which were centuries old, stories of the great mythic cycles, or others related to contemporary, local or national events. This art was a non-literary one, generally left untranscribed. Thus if we are to consider Carleton on the grounds that he transcribed these tales (with slight embellishments), then we have no context in which to place novels like *Valentine M'Clutchy, The Black Prophet*, or the several long tales like *The Poor Scholar*. These are not by any estimation exclusive transcriptions of folk-belief, though significant elements of folk-belief do appear and influence them. The character of Donnel Dhu, from *The Black Prophet*, could well be seen as coming from the ominous human shapes given form by the seanchaí's rendition, but a distinct moral motive animates Carleton. His endeavour to show to Ireland those 'debasing circumstances which prevent her from being what she ought to be' manifests itself according to the particular circumstances he chooses to write about. What 'Ireland' meant to Carleton is the key question.

He saw Ireland idealistically, as a Utopian community informed with an instinctive moral code of virtue and behaviour. This code had been severely damaged by the greed of men (or more accurately Man's greed) and their foolhardiness. He saw Ireland's ills as flowing from the personal neglect of a handful of amoral landowners, from the ignorance of English parliamentarians, from the ungodly and self-seeking activities of certain Irish politicians, their henchmen and the evil-doers of the Secret Societies, Orange or Green. Beyond this, the tide of Ireland's corruption lay in a general malaise of human nature – insolence, drink and sloth. The extreme subjectivity of Carleton's criticisms is a manifestation of his religious temperament scanning man after The Fall. It was Sin, not nascent Irish capitalism or cruel English justice, which created Ireland's woes.

In replying to the criticisms of *The Evening Mail*, which considered the granting of the Government's State pension misguided, Carleton proclaimed:

I am not now nor have I ever been at any time a repealer. I am not a Young Irelander, nor, in a political sense at least, an old one. I am no Republican, no Communist, but a plain, retiring literary man who wishes to avoid politics and to devote his future life to such works as he hopes may improve his country and elevate his people. (O'Donoghue, *The Life*, Vol. 2, p. 133. *The Evening Mail* did not publish the letter).

Carleton was fifty-four when he wrote this (1848) with most of the 'reputable' works behind him. His appeal to being 'a plain retiring literary man' rings hollow when we read in his preface to *The Tithe Proctor* of the 'degeneracy' of the Irish character and of the Irishman as:

... [a] creature of agitation – is neither honest, nor candid, nor manly, nor generous, but a poor skulking dupe, at once slavish and insolent, offensive and cowardly – who carries as a necessary consequence, the principles of political dishonesty into the practises of private life, and is consequently disingenuous and fraudulent.

The reply to the *Evening Mail* criticisms and the comments from his preface demonstrate how erratic a temperament he had. Charles Gavan Duffy, one of Carleton's close friends, berates him in a letter for 'the tempestuous fury of your own passion'. 'In a gust of passion you are one of the most unjust of men, and shut your eyes to everything but your wrath' (*The Life*, Vol. 2, p. 77).

From the early days when he could distance himself sufficiently from his work to make it artistically valuable, Carleton grew, increasingly, to view the subject of his work with contempt and to substitute literary expression with his own authoritarian voice. Caught in a confusing web of suffering and social conflict, he was ever-willing to lash out at whatever he thought to be threatening him or his beloved family. The intense subjectivity of his criticisms, his defensive recoiling and the far-flung attacks, justify us in agreeing with Duffy when he said that Carleton was incapable of understanding any formal ideology. (O'Donoghue, *The Life*, Vol. 2, p. 57). The apparently stable authorial voice of the novels is questionable: the self-identity changes throughout the novels as Carleton dons different mantles of authorial control, and often, of tyranny.

Behind the confident, assuring author-image, guiding us, like Defoe's dramatised selves, through one fictive event after another, lies Carleton's changing relationship with his readers. It is often a confused relationship, difficult to define in terms of the characters and events which he describes. Many of the problems that Carleton faced were, of course, derived from his own unstable and exposed relationship to nineteenth-century Ireland, a country prone to famine and insurrection: of a troubled and turbulent colonised society.

The violence of oppression and 'insurrection' that Carleton exposed in his earlier work is reduced, in a novel such as *The Tithe Proctor*, to indistinct generalisations about 'the state of the country'. The rhetorical impulse which animated most of what Carleton wrote finally dominates his imagination. He seems incapable of revealing, through characters and situations, a realistically fashioned world in which the effects of violence, sectarianism, hunger and social deprivation are described. As *The Tithe Proctor* shows, Carleton grew to depend almost exclusively upon sensationalism and rhetoric. The 'wrath' and 'tempestuous fury' that Gavan Duffy saw in Carleton's character actually engulfed his imagination, drawing into ever-diminishing circles the strength and impact of his literary abilities. In Carleton's constant belief that his fellow countrymen had neglected him there was also the strong suggestion that he lacked self-confidence. In letters to his daughter from London, Carleton sounds a note of incredulous surprise at the attention paid to him:

> You have no notion of my great reputation here. I could not have believed it. They place me next to Sir Walter Scott ... (O'Donoghue, *Life II*, p. 152)

Yet wavering between the extremes of self-importance and disillusionment, Carleton became withdrawn towards the end of his life and diverted most of his energies to finding posts for his sons and finance for his wife and daughters. The failure of his public readings, in Belfast in 1859, was accompanied by sickness and difficulty in seeing. His publications were erratic and his life seemed to be taken up with details and difficulties over contracts and the reprinting of earlier work.

'I have been always a poor and struggling man', he wrote, 'with large domestic claims upon me'. In the same letter, written in 1863 to his Belfast friend, Dr Corry, Carleton set out his own vision of literature in Ireland:

> The only three names which Ireland can point to with pride are Griffin's, Banim's, and – do not accuse me of vanity when I say it – my own. Banim and Griffin are gone, and I will soon follow them – *ultimus Romanorum*, and after that will come a lull, an obscurity of perhaps half a century, when a new condition of civil society and a new phase of manners and habits among the people – for this is a transition period – may introduce new fields and new tastes for other writers, for in this manner the cycles of literature and taste appear, hold their day, displace each other, and make room for others.

The tone of objectivity in this passage conceals the 'tired and exhausted' state Carleton had reached. Six years later he died, aged seventy-five.

◆

Assessments of Carleton's literary achievement have varied. The dominant note of criticism has stressed the sociological factors which shaped his work. Little attention has been paid to the actual literary ability that Carleton displayed.

A rather circular logic attends much that has been written about Carleton. From his peasant origins, Carleton is viewed as recording the peasants' life and on this basis alone his work is held to be deserving of praise. Clearly a critical perspective based on such subjective grounds advance neither our understanding of Irish literature nor engages with the social and cultural conditions which has determined its development.

Writing on this subject, Frank O'Connor said that Carleton's 'life story is fascinating because from it we see an extraordinary natural genius being first directed then diverted and finally frustrated by outside circumstances'. (Frank O'Connor, *The Backward Look*, p. 138). O'Connor maintained that to have 'succeeded in London was almost to have forgotten Ireland' but that success in Ireland 'was almost to have ignored Europe'. The 'lack of a literate audience',

O'Connor concluded, crippled the literature of Ireland during the nineteenth century. It is from this position that several critics have assumed that Ireland lacked a middle-class, the 'literate audience', and consequently the conventional relationship between author and audience was absent. As one survey of nineteenth-century Anglo-Irish literature put it:

> ... the kind of shared understanding between the author and his readers implicit in the English situation did not pertain for Carleton and his audience. Thus, the attempt to represent Irish reality and then to draw conclusions about it which were appropriate to the sensibility of nineteenth-century English society destroyed all unity of style.
>
> (Pepy Barlow, and others. 'The Anglo-Irish Novel', *The Education Times*, 11 April 1974).

On the contrary, Ireland did have a middle-class during the nineteenth century, as shown in Joseph Lee's *The Modernisation of Ireland* (Dublin, 1974), while other sources suggest that the Irish middle-class was, if not as substantial as the English middle-class, a literate and culturally aware section of society. (See, for instance, Bayle Bernard, *The Life of Samuel Lover*, 2 vols., London, 1874.) The number of magazines, ranging from the *Dublin University Magazine* to Duffy's *Hibernia Magazine*, and the activity of Irish publishers, imply some degree of a cultured reading public. Furthermore, the political bias and cultural ambitions of *The Nation* and the Young Ireland movement, generally taken as the populist voice of peasant radicalism, was more often the articulation of middle-class dissent, a point made by Malcolm Brown in *The Politics of Irish Literature* (pp. 27, 32, 55-57,109).

Carleton's stories and novels are not solely direct addresses to English 'governors'; they deal explicitly with the reasons why the 'independent' farmer, the personification of the rural middle-class, was being driven off the land. If one recalls the signatories of Carleton's pension testimonial, the list presents the professional Catholic middle-class as well as the Protestant landed gentry.

In neglecting to note the presence of a middle-class, critics have found a ready-made but mechanical explanation for the uneven development of Irish literature in English during the nineteenth century. The particular shape of this development should be viewed from the background, artistic concerns and social motivations of the individual authors themselves. This does not mean reducing the important influences of social and cultural conditions upon the personal development of an author; or on the growth of Irish literature in general. The matrix of personal, cultural and social factors which is the basis of all literature is exceptionally complex and cannot be superficially related to the political exigencies of a particular time and place. This for instance is the literary and cultural critic Daniel Corkery at a very weak moment:

> *Castle Rackrent* ... lives by English suffrage, but Gerald Griffin's *The Collegians* lives by Irish suffrage ... the work of Somerville and Ross lives mostly by English suffrage; while Carleton's work – written quite obviously under Ascendancy influence – lives by Irish suffrage ...

The 'suffrage' of an author, whether it be Edgeworth or Carleton, lives and retains interest because of its value and merit as a work of art. Taste and prejudice may determine the availability of an author's work but that is an entirely different matter.

Carleton's strengths and faults as an author are related to various factors. His concern to show that the contradictions in Irish society could be overcome often led to the weakening of a convincing portrayal of character and the uneven management of plot. Notwithstanding this failure, Carleton possessed special insights into the early period of nineteenth-century living in Ireland. As a 'social' novelist, Carleton can be seen fighting a rearguard action against those forces which he considered disruptive of Irish life. Carleton misunderstood and, in his novels, misinterpreted the great thrust of the peasant movements which, under the leadership of men like O'Connell, were on the march toward democracy in Ireland. Thinking always of an ideal Ireland in which the painful experiences of his early childhood and boyhood would be banished and its joys would dominate, Carleton reacted bitterly to the insistent shattering of his dream. As the contradictions within Irish society shot violently to the surface of everyday life, Carleton tried to contain them by returning to his own past as a means of imaginatively stabilising the effects of contemporary violence upon his idealistic vision of landlord and tenant harmony. Inevitably, the imaginative pattern he had established, for example in *Traits and Stories*, proved insufficient to sustain the greater artistic and stylistic demands which the writing of novels demanded. In *Traits and Stories* Carleton worked through the 'raw material' of his early experience upon which the novels were also to depend. From the initially ambivalent and ironic attitude of early stories like 'The Battle of the Factions', Carleton moved towards the characterisation of figures who were representative of 'enlightened views'.

Carleton had tried to become a respectable writer, an 'early Victorian', but the passionate and disillusioned Irish novelist never quite succeeded. It is significant that Carleton greatly admired Thackeray's work 'more than those of any English contemporary' (*Life II*, p. 157). As Frank O'Connor said: 'Carleton himself could not accept that anonymous folk artistry' (*The Backward Look*, p. 138). Perhaps his cultural background, with its tradition of 'aesthetic irresponsibility' and the powerful sense of *in extremis*, militated against his personal desire to be seen as the contemplative man of letters, the 'Walter Scott of Ireland', as he was pleased to be called. Certainly the novels bear the mark of personal frustration, even defeat; there is a deep sense of insecurity at the very centre of his writing. To the end of his days, Carleton felt that the Irish people had not stood by him and that, in spite of his success elsewhere, the Irish had not voiced their appreciation of what he had laboured to do on their behalf. This is possibly what Anthony Cronin had in mind when he suggests that:

> ... there seems at times to be a feeling of entrapment in Carleton, and a very real and personal fear of certain forces for the precise reason he is drawn to them. (*The Irish Times*, 5 April 1974)

Carleton's 'sense of the frightfulness of certain forces', which Cronin relates to 'his feeling of entrapment', are the forces of violence, land and religion. For Carleton, as 'perhaps' for Joyce's Stephen, 'history is a nightmare from which one must struggle to awake'. The rhetorical similarity between Stephen Dedalus's diary entry at the close of *A Portrait of an Artist as a Young Man* and the direct moral emphases of Carleton's prefaces and many passages in his work is a fascinating comparison. Carleton was to some extent a victim of circumstances beyond his control. The tremendous pressure of immediate circumstances like famine and sectarian outrage ultimately undermined his imaginative power. As he remarked in the 'Author's Preface' to *The Black Prophet*:

> ... do not the workings of death and desolation among us in the present time give them a fearful corroboration, and prove how far the strongest imagery of fiction is frequently transcended by the terrible realities of Truth?

For Joyce the 'nightmare' of history presented a kind of challenge to his creative resilience and one which he responded to imaginatively with the reserves of European culture at his disposal. The paradoxes and passions which were the obsessions of Joyce's mind became in his art the dramatised conscience of Irish experience. Carleton never achieved that degree of heightened imaginative self-consciousness. When one looks at his work, one sees, as Walter Allen saw in relation to Sir Walter Scott, 'one vast work ... one great epic picture'. It is a canvas rich in colour and scale but lacking in complexity. The 'bizarre, non-rational, sometimes lunatic figures' that 'haunt' Scott's novels are similar to those in Carleton's work: Paddy Devaun, Fardorougha, Raymond-na-hattha, Poll Dollin, the Black Prophet and Skinadre. Yet Carleton's 'genteel' characters, such as the Returned Gentleman, the responsible landowners and the women figures, are all invariably one-dimensional and lifeless. It is through the pathetic, violent and brutalised peasant characters that Carleton presents us with a stunning revelation of Irish life during the early nineteenth century. These figures, like Devlin in Phelim O'Toole's match-making, articulate the paradoxical nature of that peasant society we have still such difficulty with in Ireland today. Between the extreme swings of the emotional pendulum, Carleton tried to create examples of stability and security. His failure, manifest in the superficial characterisation of the 'good' figures, was to realise that the seemingly intractable contradictions of Irish society had led inevitably to violence and recurrent social outrage. Confining his energies to the search for stability, both personal and social, Carleton's creative work was burdened with a moral freight few novelists could sustain.

Carleton's historical position can overwhelm our critical understanding of his literary accomplishment. As he was only too aware, he was writing in a transitional state. Irish society had experienced, and its literature had expressed, tremendous social and political upheavals, as well as the apocalyptic Famine. The patterns and traumas of Irish peasant life emerge from a reading of Carleton's work as they do in no other writer of his time. The complex linguistic transition from Irish to English is presented in close relation to the vernacular speech of the peasants. This pattern is one of Carleton's major accomplishments. Carleton also expressed the constant presence in the lives of his peasant characters of sectarianism, famine and violence.

In a 'final assessment' of Carleton's work one must, however, record his personal courageous endeavour to speak for the inarticulate suffering and grief of the Irish peasant. It is this attribute in the man and in the work that strikes us with the greatest force. In attempting to find an imaginative order to the turbulent years between 1830 and 1850, Carleton grappled with his 'barbarous knowledge' but never quite found a consistently authentic means of expression. Whatever faults one may find in the work, Carleton as a man exhibited an integrity and courage which kept him, often wrongly, firm in the belief that what he was saying about the Irish people was important and capable of influencing their actions and beliefs.

Carleton's writing career is salutatory in more ways than one. Carleton's address to the people began with a search for authenticity, ended with a frozen reputation but maintained throughout an integrity during unparalleled times of anguish.

Yet, in an artistic sense, he succumbed to stereotypical images of his own people and it is a problem still very much with us.

[1994]

# MINDSTUFF ON MacNEICE

At two Irish literature conferences I have attended in recent years, it struck me as curious that Louis MacNeice's name was rarely mentioned. It bothered me, not because MacNeice has suffered neglect as a poet but rather for what it said about the present state of critical readings in Irish poetry. The crunch came when, at the second of the conferences, an undoubtedly well-intentioned academic quoted, in his lecture, Michael Longley's closing statement in *A Neolithic Night: A Note on the Irishness of Louis MacNeice*:

> Ireland must be one of the very few remaining areas in the English-speaking world which are still likely to produce poets who write out of a response to religion.
>
> *Two Decades of Irish Writing* (1975)

The fact that Longley was referring specifically to Louis MacNeice ('The vividness of MacNeice's work was projected partly as an assault on religious narrowness and cultural restriction') was somehow overlooked while the 'response to religion', perhaps unselfconsciously, took the shape of an essentially Irish and Catholic preoccupation in the lecturer's talk.

It would be, of course, a benign oversight were it not for what it tells us about the categories of perception and critical assumptions that underwrite much, if not all, of the current discussion about contemporary Irish poetry.

While the principles which govern influence and artistic patrimony largely go unexamined, the dominant lines are well-entrenched by now and I see no point in rehearsing them again here. However, in spite of the critical presence of Yeats as the pivotal point in such discussion, MacNeice's original work (1941) on Yeats is rarely mentioned. Similarly, little attention has been given to his other varied and useful writing, from *Modern Poetry* (1938) to *Varieties of Parable* (1965); both texts are out of print. Alan Heuser's edition of the *Selected Criticism of Louis MacNeice* (Oxford 1987) is, therefore, more than timely, ranging from a review of *Auden's Poems* (1931) to the poignant note MacNeice wrote for the *Poetry Book Society Bulletin* about *The Burning Perch*, just over a week before he died on 3 September 1963:

> Fear and resentment seem here to be serving me in the same way as Yeats in his old age claimed to be served by 'lust and rage', and yet I had been equally fearful and resentful of the world we live in when I was writing *Solstices* (1961).

*Selected Literary Criticism* (1987) reveals how MacNeice thought about what he was doing and the way in which he probed his own artistic identity through other poets' work and by questioning more abstract issues, as in *Experience with Images* (1949). Perhaps MacNeice was too available, too aware, as Heuser describes, of 'non-transcendence, of prose, a common-sense earthy reality'. Yet his world was 'transformed by psychic types and scenes out of dream, fantasy, myth; the imagination alive within him from childhood, from boyhood readings of saga, epic, romance, and the picaresque. Anchored in the facts of waking life but prey to dream and nightmare, he recognised the dream logic of story ...' Heuser continues:

> Mythic pattern and dream rhythm penetrated the prison of an honest prose world with hovering psychic truths either as paradoxes or anomalies or as genuine double vision which he was keen to point out and defend ...

MacNeice's prose is rarely valuable in itself. He is not a stylist when it comes to telling his reader what's what. He lacks the ease and the facility of the professional trend-spotter, probably because what he writes about actually means a lot to him. Indeed, as MacNeice tackles various set-pieces, like 'Poetry Today' (1935) or 'Subject in Modern Poetry' (1937), there is a good deal of covert justification going on that suggests a persistent thorn of self-doubt: Why be a poet? What can it mean?

Given the opportunity to confute conventional wisdom and orthodoxy, as in his essay 'Poetry Today', MacNeice is, in typical fashion, subdued but lethal:

> Mr. Michael Roberts has given a reason why poets are ceasing to write free verse. But many intelligent people cannot see why they began to write it. The plea is sometimes made that free verse is an attempt to express the quickened and irregular tempo of modern life. This explanation is vague and bad (like most explanations which hinge on the word 'express').

In 'Subject in Modern Poetry', MacNeice comes closest in this volume to revealing his own sense of what being a poet entails; it is a kind of provocative personae-deflation:

> ... poets have ceased showing themselves off as mere poets. They have better things to do; they are writing about things again.

Later in the same essay, when tracing the relation to life of twentieth-century poetry (his phrase), MacNeice remarks:

> If we do not count the War, when War poems such as those of Sassoon had a large public, poetry subsequently became less popular the nearer it came to life. This was because in its endeavour to be true it became very difficult.

As John Lucas has said of Robert Graves' 'decorum', it 'could be offered as very English, as ways of not making a song-and-dance about poetry' (*Modern English Poetry*, 1986). I think there are elements in MacNeice's personality as an artist which are perceived, in the same sense as Graves', to be 'very English' and hence unsympathetic to the canon of Irish literature, policed as it so often is by the prejudice of familiarity and caricature: 'Poets have ceased showing themselves off as mere poets', writes MacNeice, and '... poetry ... became less popular the nearer it came to life'.

Both points MacNeice upholds are immediately suspect in an Irish context where poets are expected to perform 'as poets' and difficulty in poetry is generally seen as an elitist contempt for 'popularity' – i.e. finding favour with the people. As MacNeice makes abundantly clear in the following quotation, from 'Subject in Modern Poetry', he had a fair idea of what can happen when poets write out of 'an accredited theme', to use Samuel Beckett's phrase of the 1930s:

Then came Mr. T. S. Eliot – the arch highbrow. But the arch highbrow writing down honestly his own view of the world is a more human, 'popular' and valuable person than the purveyor of 'poetic' subjects to a public which buys them because they are the accepted things; just as they once bought antimacassars and now buy chromium-plated clocks with unreadable dials. Mr. Eliot was, indeed, extraordinarily (pathologically?) interested in literature, but he never fixed a great gulf between the street and the classics; he saw them in inter-relation.

There is a weight of knowledge in this passage, an understanding which belongs in the world, and also, under the surface, a sense of anger at the vanity of human wishes (those antimacassars, the unreadable clocks) which reveals MacNeice's truly great virtue as a poet and, probably, also as a man. It shows itself continually throughout the awkward, adamant and restless prose of *Selected Literary Criticism*, turning up epigrammatic gems ('... if a poet is to write at all, he should be content with the results proper to poetry. If he wants yoga he can go elsewhere') or crystallising into the stated case, such as the following, written in 1940:

Art, though as much conditioned by material factors as anything else, is a manifestation of human freedom. The artist's freedom connoted honesty because a lie, however useful in politics, hampers artistic vision.

MacNeice's understanding of literature unravels, too, several conundrums, as when he refers to Lawrence as a writer who 'had imagination without common sense – and got away with it – but for most people this divorce will degrade imagination itself'. There are some points made which should be lodged at the back of every person's mind who writes, or writes about, poetry:

Verse is a precision instrument and owes its precision very largely to the many and subtle differences which an ordinary word can acquire from its place in a rhythmical scheme.

This leaves us at the real beginnings and also at the unpredictable consummation of poetry as a form of art. Why MacNeice's experience, knowledge and accomplishment are not better known and studied in Ireland makes for a very complicated story indeed.

## II

Poets are often better known by the friends they keep than by what they have written. Critics are happiest with eras. Individuals cause problems. The great shape of 'Themes' and 'Literary Periods' and the identifying of both that passes for much literary criticism are regularly fouled up in the muddy water of an individual poet's life and work. It is, quite simply, grander to talk about 'The War Poets', 'The 1930s', 'The Movement', than it is to consider Larkin in Hull, W. S. Graham in Cornwall or MacNeice in London. They are, instead, counters in a critical game of chessboard manoeuvres about 'Influence', 'Literary Identity', 'Nationality'. Somehow their being poets evaporates. This goes against the grain of everything that Louis MacNeice believed the function of poetry to be:

> The poet is a maker, not a retail trader. The writer today should be not so much the mouthpiece of a community (for he will only tell it what it knows already) as its conscience, its critical faculty, its generous instinct.

MacNeice was an opponent of determinism in any shape or form. It represented to him claustrophobia or the snuffing out of possibility, and underneath the political stance, which he called 'myths of themselves', he detected literary postures in several of his peers. In this sense MacNeice was ahead of his time (or before it), seeing the danger 'of a poetry which will be judged by its party colours'. He went on to state, in 'Poetry Today':

> Bourgeois poetry is assumed to have been found wanting; the only alternative is communist poetry. This seems to be an over-simplification. I doubt whether communist and bourgeois are exclusive alternatives in the arts, and if they are, I suspect these would-be communist poets of playing to the bourgeoisie.

His ability to expose the sham (the pinpointed accusation in the sentence quoted above) had its roots in his upbringing, for Ulster is a place that has no time for pretensions of a 'literary' sort and where culture is naturally mixed with politics. In tracing this inbred matrix throughout MacNeice's prolific sensibility, Edna Longley has done a marvellous job in *Louis MacNeice: A Study*. Nothing is left to chance in her book and next to nothing can be misinterpreted. This no-nonsense approach accords with MacNeice's own criticism and one perceives a meeting of minds in this fine study.

Ms. Longley sees what MacNeice meant when he wrote about 'where literature ends and real politics begins'. She links his realism with the North: 'These shades of the Ulster prison house illustrate how the timeless 'moments of glory' in MacNeice's poetry are accentuated by an ineradicable awareness of their opposite...'

When she quotes MacNeice's recollection of his schooldays at Sherborne: '... the boys ... seemed suddenly terribly young; I had learned their language, but they could not learn mine, could never breathe my darkness', the self-awareness is shocking.

It is this darkness, a fecund, terrible unshakeable darkness that clouds MacNeice's poetry and, as Michael Longley points out in his brisk introduction to the *Selected Poems*, drives MacNeice's imagination towards the light. While fighting shy of Lawrentian passion, MacNeice knew the emotional and spiritual cost of this darkness; it was no acquired faddish posture (although the image of 'The Brandy Glass' or 'Bagpipe Music' has perhaps carried readers too far away in another, jazzy, direction).

As Edna Longley remarks:

> The politics of MacNeice's Irish poems begin in childhood because Irish politics begin with the family and not at voting age. Hence the deeper sedimentation of his political awareness than was usual among English writers during the 1930s.

What Ireland meant to MacNeice, what destabilising effect it had upon his imagination, can be compared with the experience of working-class life in Lawrence. Both writers did not have to search for discontent or 'issues'; they were born into them. This meant that MacNeice, like Orwell, 'was not only amused but frightened by the surrender of intellectuals to totalitarian habits of mind, to strange imperatives'. And it was this 'surrender' that led the intellectual, in MacNeice's opinion, to forget 'the end in the means, the evil of the means drowns the good of the end, power corrupts, the living gospel withers, Siberia fills with ghosts'.

Accordingly, Longley suggests, MacNeice's *Autumn Journal* 'found a political role for poetry in criticising the effect of politics on language' and throughout his work he 'emphasised ... not how poetry might help to change society, but how a sense of social obligation might change poetry'. How he balanced these conflicting claims of poetry and politics and his own 'sense of social obligation' is well charted in *Louis MacNeice: A Study*. One cannot, however, avoid the sense of MacNeice as a man haunted by the dark side of Irish life, the North specifically, its repressiveness (sexual as much as emotional), the puritan assertiveness, the cheery demeanour in the face of life's permissible limits. He knew these things at first hand. They were part of him and were both his strength and his weakness.

On the one hand MacNeice sought, like Joyce but without his fanaticism, to fly these nets. On the other hand, he confronted them poetically. This confrontation broke in many directions but, in Irish terms, they led towards his glamorising of an always external west of Ireland (even while he saw its underside); or they led towards those remarkable, chilly poems which Michael Longley has identified as MacNeice's greatest.

These are the poems which trace the jagged edges of dream and nightmare, hovering before light, or rain, as morning washes clear the fears and uncertainties of night. If there is a formal quality to MacNeice's celebrations, like a fixed smile, then it is because of a profound loneliness in the man which his poetry embodies.

This is the loneliness, and even spiritual homelessness, that comes from his background in Protestant Ulster. For no matter in what ways MacNeice could distance himself from its worst excesses (either through imagined genealogies or imaginative rebuttals), the fact is that his upbringing fundamentally defined his self. MacNeice's poetry is an exemplary and determined struggle with this inheritance and one which deserves an extended study. Yet it is this very 'point' that has obscured MacNeice's significance and led to much confusion.

When, for instance, Seamus Heaney in 'The Placeless Heaven: Another Look at Kavanagh' (*The Government of the Tongue*) describes MacNeice's poems as 'a mind-stuff [that] existed in a cultural setting which was at one remove from me and what I came from', he is being true to himself, while forgetting the profound, aching sense of separation in MacNeice:

> I envied them, of course [Heaney writes] their security in the big world of history and poetry which happened out there, far beyond the world of state scholarships, the Gaelic Athletic Association, October devotions, the Clancy brothers, buckets and eggboxes where I had had my being.

But it is within MacNeice that the insecurity lies, and his ability to live with it is the hallmark of his personal courage as a man and poet. The created masks of the cosmopolitan, the Anglo accent, the man about town, are frail compensation for that abiding sense of rootedness in familial, social and cultural terms that characterises Kavanagh and, indeed, Heaney. Yet, ironically, both Kavanagh and MacNeice enter a similar loneliness which Edna Longley refers to when she quotes Geoffrey Grigson, from *New Verse* (Autumn 1938):

> The only justified retreat is the loneliness from which everything and everybody is more visible, the loneliness in the centre and not on the edge. What we need now is not the fanatic, but the critical moralist, and the one loneliness which is justified is Rilke's loneliness surrounded by everything thorough, exact, without slovenliness, impressionable and honest.

MacNeice does not perform on the edge, as perhaps Irish poets are customarily expected to, for he embodies Grigson's rather haughty prescription to the letter.

There is in MacNeice's poetry that existential clarity that one associates with Camus or, in a much less poetically burdened way, with Montale, or even Beckett. MacNeice was, in this strict sense, a child of his time but emphatically not in the conventional way in which one reads of 'the Auden Generation'.

That fiction and the quality of fake (or *kitsch*, in Milan Kundera's lexicon) which Auden converted into mocking parable and fun never really surfaced in MacNeice, despite his best efforts. He was perilously honest with himself as a poet and, rather than taking time to sort things out (between the late 1940s to the 1950s when he was plainly 'dulled by the dull stretches' as Michael Longley puts it), MacNeice tried to write his way into a new territory of experience and expression. This eventually worked and there can be little doubt about the value of *Solstices* (1961) and *The Burning Perch* (1963) or, indeed, of the collection of lectures, *Varieties of Parable* (1965).

In his unfinished autobiography, *The Strings Are False*, MacNeice recounts the following scene:

> So I got on to this boat and here I am, fitted with a gas-mask carrying my lifebelt from cabin to lounge to dining room, watching the airmen who are more than young drink their pints of beer or listening to someone at the piano around the corner picking out with one finger *Land of Hope and Glory* or to a mouth-organ playing *The Rose of Tralee*. It is, as I said, the same boat that brought me over [to the US]. That was in January 1940 and this is December 1940. But before all that? I am 33 years old and what can I have been doing that I still am in a muddle? But everyone else is too, maybe our muddles are concurrent. Maybe, if I look back, I shall find that my life is not just mine, that it mirrors the lives of others – or shall I say the Life of the Other? Anyway I will look back. And return to pick up the present, or rather to pick up the future.

Like his life, the cause of his premature death tells of a man constantly in search of authenticity, too willing perhaps to explain himself and the country he came from but unafraid in his belief that this is what a poet should do:

> By a high star our course is set,
> Our end is Life. Put out to sea.

[1987–1988]

# THE WORLD AS PROVINCE:
## MacGreevy, Devlin and Coffey

It is not uncommon for writers to receive recognition first away from their home. The obvious example is Joyce and after him, Beckett. For while they were well known to a floating circle of writers in the Ireland of their time, their reputations rest upon other grounds – a relentless certainty that what mattered to them was their writing and the unshakable faith that it would, eventually, find its own level in terms of general and critical understanding. They were to see this happening in their own lifetimes, particularly Beckett, whose wearisome uneasiness with the public show of writing became legendary.

Thomas MacGreevy (1893–1967) praised and known by both Joyce and Beckett, has lived in a kind of critical limbo since the publication of his *Poems* (1934). Between then and Thomas Dillon Redshaw's edition of *Collected Poems* (1971), MacGreevy's poetry has popped up in various anthologies, but without the pioneering attention given to MacGreevy by Michael Smith's *Lace Curtain* magazine and his New Writers' Press, it is more than likely that we would not now have a definitive *Collected Poems*, edited by Susan Schreibman.

MacGreevy remains an unknown quantity, his name bandied around as a linkman between Joyce, Beckett and other writers from Ireland, such as Brian Coffey and Denis Devlin, a 'group' of writers whose inclination was away from the 'Victorian gaeldom' of Yeats' revivalism – by the late 1920s in a state of terminal decline – towards Paris and the hub of continental experimentalism. Indeed, like Beckett, MacGreevy spent quite some time travelling in Europe and the two were to remain close friends (mainly through correspondence) for life.

At the age of 17, MacGreevy moved from his family's home in Tarbert, Co. Kerry to Dublin and, in 1911, transferred to London where he worked in the Civil Service. He joined the British Army in 1917 and served as a gunner in Ypres and on the Somme. Demobbed, he went to Trinity College, studied political science and history, travelled through Spain, Switzerland and thence to London again (1924) and Paris. MacGreevy worked there as a *lecteur* at the École Normale Supérieure before, under Joyce's influence, he took up an editorial post with the English edition of a journal of the fine arts, *Formes*. He returned to London in 1933 before settling back in Dublin in 1941.

Throughout these twenty-odd years, MacGreevy lived by his wits as part-time lecturer (in Paris, but also at the National Gallery, London, until the Second World War broke out), literary journalist, critic and translator. The period marks publication of a series of monographs along with criticism in many of the leading journals of the time.

This remarkable poetic and critical vitality barely survives, however, into the 1940s. So by the time MacGreevy has taken on responsibility as director of the National Gallery of Ireland in 1950, his poetic output has all but ceased. In 1955, he begins his *Memoirs* and, in spite of increasing ill-health, completes a study of Nicolas Poussin, published by the Dolmen Press in 1960. Retiring from the National Gallery in 1963, he died four years later, in his seventy-fourth year.

The central issue concerning MacGreevy's life as an artist is the point which gathers together all this remarkable work as critic and gallery-man – his fall into poetic silence. Certainly Schreibman in the introduction takes us towards that conclusion.

On the one hand, there is the praise for *Poems* (1934) from Beckett and Wallace Stevens, among others. On the other hand, the dozen poems he was to write in the thirty years between then and his death, testify to a set of circumstances which he could not creatively overcome.

Ms. Schreibman assembles the arguments as follows. According to Mervyn Wall, MacGreevy simply 'ran out of inspiration'; but, in his *Memoirs*, he identifies 'economic circumstances ... psychological make-up' and suggests he was interested in 'living' rather than writing. Schreibman hints at other factors: 'the reception of *Poems* in Dublin' of the time and sets this beside the 'larger problem facing an Irish artist or writer working in the early decades of the century'.

But how does this fit? After all, MacGreevy was *away* for quite some time, and what about the lesson he must surely have learnt from Joyce, the supportive friendship of many, such as Charles Prentice at Chatto & Windus, or George Reavey, translator and publisher of Europa Press; the dismissive silence that greeted much of Beckett's early work and *his* struggle to find publishers, or the dedicated example of younger writers such as Denis Devlin or Brian Coffey? MacGreevy was part of the literary action of the time. He was on speaking terms with important figures like Eliot and Herbert Read.

The editor of *Collected Poems* insists, though, upon 'the sense of the indigenous artist's dilemma in a colonial world' as going some way to explaining 'MacGreevy's unwillingness to risk presenting his talents to the Dublin of his time' and concludes that the reasons for his 'failure to continue to write poetry' touch 'upon the condition of Irish poets in a (post) colonial world'. Where does this leave Devlin, Coffey, Beckett, Clarke, Kavanagh, O'Faoláin, or Louis MacNeice and John Hewitt since, when viewed throughout their entire working lives, one sees an unstoppable flow of writing, in spite of the prolonged silences Clarke and Coffey experienced between publications?

Undoubtedly, the economic difficulties led MacGreevy into pouring effort into writing that *paid*. Nothing unusual in this; writers in Ireland and elsewhere (colonised or coloniser) live as best they can on what they can. The poet in MacGreevy seems, however, to have been overwhelmed by the official public state of Irish letters which, in Dublin of the '40s and later, had little interest in the imaginative discipline and artistic lifestyle associated with the cosmopolitan ethos of a Paris or London. The devout Catholic in the man was possibly the more dominant factor when MacGreevy settled himself back into Irish society. So that, while he could see the Literary Revival for the (enabling) fiction it was in Yeats' time, the cultural and political conditions obtaining in Emergency Ireland had little space for *any* artist's dilemma.

MacGreevy must have had the time of his life in Paris during the '20s and '30s. The wonder is why he bothered to come back. A key to the reason is found in the following extract that Susan Schreibman quotes from the *Memoirs*:

> When, for a time at the Ecole Normale in Paris and later, for a short period at the hotel in the Quarter, Samuel Beckett and I had adjoining rooms and breakfasted together, Sam could go straight from his morning tea or coffee to his typewriter or his books, his biblical concordance, his dictionaries, his Stendhal. I, on the contrary, had to go out and make sure that the world was where I had left it the evening before.

Survivor of Ypres and the Somme, twice-wounded, here he was ten years on in Paris, hardly able to believe his luck. And who would blame him? But was 'Ireland' to blame for the returned exile's silence? In which case, whatever happened to artfulness, the Joycean cunning?

Ms. Schreibman's unfussy annotations give us the poems upon which the important literary discriminations will be made now that, at long last, MacGreevy's poems are available again. Readers will be able to make their own minds up about this vulnerable and yearning artistic talent, at odds with itself for most of the time:

> The light green, touched with gold
> Of clusters of grapes;
> And, crouching at the foot of a renaissance wall,
> A little cupid, in whitening stone,
> Weeping over a lost poetry.

## II

It can become very easy to forget about individual poets when one hears and reads so much about 'Irish Poetry'. There is, after all, a trail of amenable phrases and slogans referring to 'Irish Poetry' that cannot be directed at the specific, all-too-human figure of the poet.

'A standing army', from Kavanagh, has had quite a long life, bringing to mind a patronising sense of combat, a marshalled unity of purpose, the poor old infighting literary community.

There are, however, several poets this century in Ireland who seem to stand above or beyond the imagined fray. Not so much aloof as oblivious, going about their business. Denis Devlin is one of them. As James Mays remarks in the Dedalus edition of *Collected Poems*, Devlin's poetry rebukes any sense of 'programmatic understanding'. On the contrary, it is illustrated by those authors 'who evidently meant most to Devlin: Hopkins, Racine, Seeve, Montaigne'. This catholicism of taste, and openness, is one of the most appealing qualities in Devlin.

Again, James Mays makes the telling point when, in referring to writers (Laura Riding, Hugh MacDiarmid, Christopher Middleton) who 'in our time have … stood apart and argued for a more ample understanding of poetry', he suggests that 'what sets Devlin at a distance from them is the way they have been marked by their isolation. They have all in some way been maimed by their failure to win recognition. Devlin was not because, from the beginning, his poetry engaged the world differently, on terms which had simultaneously more to do with private need and utterly impersonal ambitions'.

That last sentence should be etched in the mind of every young (and not-so-young) poet writing in Ireland today. In Irish literary culture the emphasis all too often falls upon the personality of the poet instead of where it rightly belongs – with the poetry. What makes Denis Devlin such an important figure *now* is the example he offers of a masterly poet, in the style of the Greek Seferis or the French St. John Perse, pursuing his professional life (as a diplomat) while simultaneously retaining a fundamental commitment to the life of art. There is no ideological contradiction here. The poet and the poem are out in the world, sustained by those 'impersonal ambitions' of art, not cloistered within a self-serving clique or stage-managing a 'reputation'.

Literature in Ireland often seems like an inordinately claustrophobic affair of family squabbles, with their assumed intimacies of knowing who's who and what's what. Part of this energy accounts, after all, for some of the great interest shown abroad in Irish literature. From the young Joyce looking down his nose at the patrician Yeats, to O'Casey squaring up to the Old Man himself; Beckett falling out of Ireland, to the marauding figure of Behan or Kavanagh's castigation of Dublin, and so forth; these caricatures can get in the way though, and not only with the 'foreign' reader or writer or student.

These personalised clichés are what many in Ireland have grown to associate with their own literature, like those images of this poet or that playwright on the walls of a pub. Familiarity breeds a contempt of sorts, so what a writer actually wrote (rather than the stories he told, or where he drank) gets lost somewhere along the line.

Such a fate is particularly damning for a poet of profoundly private intensities, like Denis Devlin, whose work, in the media-lit literary world, is generally perceived in terms of 'obscurity'. As his friend, editor and fellow-poet Brian Coffey said in 1963, 'obscurity ... once used about a poet has such a burr-like quality of sticking with bad effects on his reputation and on his sales' that it is necessary to place any 'difficulty of meaning' as arises in Devlin's case 'in the correct perspective of his work as a whole'. James Mays remarks:

> Devlin appears very early to have possessed a kind of self-confidence and sense of self-determination that did not need either to follow fashion or to surround itself with the sense of belonging to a school. He remains somewhat aloof from the writers he acknowledged.

*Collected Poems* takes the reader through Devlin's poetry from *Intercessions* (1937), some uncollected early poems and translations of the '30s (from Nerval, for example); Devlin's substantial 1949 collection, *Lough Derg and Other Poems*, published in the United States; his translations of fellow-diplomat St. John Perse's *Exile and Other Poems*, towards later poems (1946–59), like the ambitious *The Heavenly Foreigner*, the delicately sensuous love poem, 'The Colours of Love', the sequences of 'The Passion of Christ' and 'Memoirs of a Turcoman Diplomat', before concluding with various uncollected poems and a translation of *Nineteen Poems* by Réné Char.

The obvious European experience and orientation of Devlin's imaginative ideals, and the fact that he published mostly in American or Italian literary journals, may well have proved too much of an obstacle for a wider audience in the closed shop of the Ireland of the Emergency and after. As a result of that critical absence, Devlin, like other poets of his generation, has been known more by the few than by the many, and more outside Ireland than within. Again, Mays points out that Devlin's 'reputation in Ireland as an experimental and difficult writer is for the large part an accident. The diplomatic career which took him abroad made it too easy to dismiss or champion him as an "international" writer'. Thirty years after his death, things may now have changed sufficiently to accommodate Denis Devlin, as he sought, in Mays's words, 'to take the world as his province'.

A little like the renewed interest of recent years in the English poet, David Gascoyne, whom he resembles in some ways, the playful poetic rhetoric of Devlin's early experimentation with surrealism might also find a sympathetic hearing today.

Similarly, Devlin's encounters with 'The poor in spirit on their rosary rounds' in Lough Derg, his portrait of Ank'hor Vat, or the Hitlerian spring in 'Little Elegy' bring us close to the vigorous and unyielding vision of Hart Crane and Joseph Brodsky, since each of these poets is a strict *maker* of language. There are, too, surroundings that seem to anticipate the languour of magic realism, as in 'Memoirs of a Turcoman Diplomat', while the setting of 'Anapolis', capital of Maryland and site of the US Naval Academy, speaks of those brave new worlds we are accustomed to recognising as our global province:

> Cadets conduct
> Camera-fans to the Governor's Residence
> To the Capitol and the Revolutionary General
> Leading ghosts on his enthusiastic stone horse.

Mays hits the nail on the head with his comment that 'poetry is more than words on the page, that poetry comes into existence as a part of a repertory'. Devlin has 'suffered' as a result; his name used (instead of his poetry being read) in a rather pointless argument about modernism and its poetic value in Ireland. Perhaps with this volume of *Collected Poems*, the critical context will emerge in which to read Devlin's world alongside the allied freedom which such a possibility, by itself, permits in 'allowing for' different kinds of poetry and alternative images of the Poet.

In contrast to what has often been said of Devlin's poetry – very literary, with the implications of 'elitist' – his writing is neither remote nor intoxicated with itself. The poems are inhabited by people and passion, and our sole obligation, as the editor rightly points out, is 'to master its language, its procedures, on its own terms'. Surely this is the most basic and ultimate requirement for the maker and reader of poetry, yet somehow, in Ireland, this has been short-circuited by a floorplan of where, as readers, we *should* go and what, when we get there, we should expect to see. The *Collected Poems* belittles such timidity that masquerades as cultural self-confidence.

There are any number of poems here to illustrate the resourcefulness of Devlin's imaginative range. It is this architectural grandeur, as a collection, as much as the formality and prismatic clarities of individual poems, which makes this volume such an important book. It addresses us in a complex way, through the images perhaps of *film-noir* and the political sea-changes of the past decade, in particular in Europe; the sexual frankness of which several poems here speak in mature terms; the examination of religious identity in Ireland and the cultural fall-out from such scrutiny ... And always the return to a landscape freed of the pathetic fallacy. Devlin, I think, was appalled by that kind of complacency:

> The druid elms, closed in their lost language,
> Their shoulders heavy
> With a menace not their natural own
> Rest in panic on the still canal.

If, at times, his own poetry was flawed by an overworked reaction, it is understandable since the man as the poet sought an authentic art for himself, something that achieved the texture and meaning of life. Devlin had his priorities right. The poetry is consequently convincing on those grounds alone; like Chagall or Miró, Denis Devlin creates his own terms of reference. This may also be a feature of his generation, for Denis Devlin shows with Brian Coffey an uncompromising belief in artistic self-sufficiency.

## III

Brian Coffey's *Poems and Versions 1929–1990* shakes the foundations of poetry to the very core of its being. From the French translations to his experimentalism in 'Leo', the transcendentalism of 'Advent' and the calm introspection of 'Missouri Sequence' or the earlier lyrics of *Third Person*, Coffey's work defines itself, as James Mays wrote in 1975:

> It is as if, thrown back and brooding on his own resources, the poet has chosen not to speak a language but to provide material for the reader to construct one himself.

This is the territory of Irish artists like Joyce and Beckett and also, in a different way, of poets like Mallarmé. It demands a freedom many readers baulk at and critics dismiss as artificial and foolhardy in its ambition to transfer continental feeling into the language of English – a language which cries out of our common stock of everyday sense and satisfactions for an empirical art. In perhaps his greatest poem, 'Death of Hektor' (1979), Coffey flies in the face of current poetic practices. Yet there is a coherence which makes the poem available to anyone who thinks about poetry and the world it inhabits in our time.

It is a declamatory poem that is also humble. There is a subsumed rage at 'Traditions, Scholars, Establishment well-filled heads/how, in vain, hope of the definite critic supreme'. What I enjoy about Coffey's poetry is the fact that he turns you around each word. He makes the reader accept responsibility for overall meaning, as the reinvigoration of the poem's classical theme roughly defines its context.

'Death of Hektor' allows more of Coffey to speak, however. It is a personal poem, struck on the opening note by the textual space around its speaking voice:

> Of what we are to Hektor nothing to say
> Of Hektor to us ...

This exchange (of learning) is what the poem is about, in an uncluttered lucid way. Coffey's lines are not meant to be memorised, although the opening passage stirs the bones:

> What scant return from turning back
> even a twenty year to jasmine soft wind
> friend in grove hand gentle
> in the green occasion of regret.

The lines are taut like those ropes which held Gulliver in place. Indeed, Coffey deals in similar proportions of the world as Swift – sometimes absurd, documentary and mythical. The imagination at work in 'Death of Hektor' is as contradictorily unconstrained by the dominant poetic conventions we mostly accept in these islands, as Swift's was in his time. Yet the poem is not distorted by its isolation from these support systems. Rather 'Death of Hektor' creates an imaginative freedom that asks us to wait and think; of the concluding image of catastrophe which, like Hektor's death, Coffey poses in stark terms of immeasurable human cost; and of the way Homer, the artist, 'gave us his Andromache lamenting', 'like any woman victim of any war robber of her world/her husband her child her friends her linen her pots and pans/the years it took to put a home together living against the grain/of great deeds her woman's life in her heart/much held fast word hidden for all'.

If this ending blurs a little into pathos, embodied in a peculiarly Irish rendering of Andromache, the Trojan princess, it seems to me well-founded by the temper and sharp reasoning of the poem.

The restraint and austerity with which Brian Coffey writes, even when it strains and obscures its own harmony, is a crucial contrast to be borne in mind by both writers and readers of poetry as they consider our present imaginative realities and responsibilities.

'Death of Hektor' has abundant wonder in it. Preserved in the poem's fragmented discourse is one of the more important artistic testimonies made by an Irish poet in our time – 'a vantage point in unrecorded past':

> Rise and fall   earth and water
> to and fro   waves of sea
> climate not weather to shelter land from fire
> sun-glow shapes cloud-cover    fills air
> all its benignity   swan-down for cygnets
> yet in the unhushed quiet it moves
> it moves    it flows
> wear away wear away   earth air water fire
> time like Camber sand blown a prairie fire below the dunes
>
> We can not hold time fast in our sights
> as if judging events in a moment unique
> like hill-top watcher taking Battle in at a glance
>
> We were not present to discover
> how what it was became what it is
> Nor see how one performs freely the long foreseen

[1993]

# THE PAROCHIAL IDYLL: W. R. Rodgers

There is a book to be written about the way Protestants from the North of Ireland see the rest of the country they live in. By which I probably mean 'Ireland': a fictional world rather than the actual place. For various reasons, this Ireland – as against the social, moral and political world of the Republic and/or republicanism – is an alluring ideal. It has a fantasy life of its own: musical, dreamy (alas), old-world-like; a kind of innocent state the Protestants themselves once belonged to or imagined themselves being cast out from by the ineluctable demands of the modern world. This attraction is a mix of the patronising, the genuine and the embarrassingly *kitsch* and naive. It could well be an important source Protestants will draw upon to find a new identity for themselves.

The intriguing thing about all this is that the fascination for things Irish, bordering on the voyeuristic, has been largely unexamined insofar as it relates to those writers in Ireland whose background is the Protestant North (shorthand, I know). We have read and heard a lot about differing relationships to landscape, but rarely, to my knowledge, have the sources and imaginative assumptions of writers like MacNeice, Rodgers, Hewitt or, for that matter, F. R. Higgins, been scrutinised. For they wrote out of an artistic and intellectual preoccupation shadowed by this idealised picture of Ireland, or a reaction against it. Even MacNeice, who had fairly sharp-witted purchase on what was going on around him, failed to understand the Republic (in the making and afterwards) while remarking, in his unfinished autobiography, *The Strings Are False*, on his sense of freedom at being in Dublin and his love affair with the west coast. Why should there be this double vision is not an intellectual question alone.

It is at the heart of Irish twentieth-century Romanticism; for Yeats left a powerfully pervasive legacy few escaped, particularly those poets who were vulnerable about their own cultural identity. Here was a state, established under the influence of artists such as Yeats, brought into being by other writers who had fought for it, like O'Faoláin and O'Donnell and, in the Second World War years, by default, perceived as a belligerent neighbour. The tone shifts when irritation creeps into *The Strings Are False* as the news of war breaking out reaches MacNeice in Galway. Forays are maintained from London after the war, as if returning to Ireland was re-entering the Old World – via rugby matches or the BBC radio programmes Rodgers made on Irish writers. Commissioned by Dan Davin, a book is planned which will draw MacNeice and Rodgers into a never completed project, the history of which Davin traces in his 'Memoir' in the *Collected Poems* of W. R. Rodgers.

I won't go into all the ins and outs of this sometimes gushy memoir, but it does have a representative value as far as Rodgers' poetry goes which I would like briefly to follow. It is about the greening of Rodgers. Davin describes how Rodgers had been 'recreated by Dublin' but the exchanges between the editor (Davin) and commissioned writers cast some light on my opening remarks. This is Rodgers to Davin:

> In a moment of insight (or drink) I suggested that Louis and I should devote the middle and hinging pages of the book to a pastoral hammer-and-tongs give-and take on Partition in which we might, as uncouth shepherds, say all the outrageous things which nobody dare put in urbane prose. Ireland forgives anything in poetry. Louis, I'm glad, likes the idea.

As the two traipse around Ireland, it becomes obvious that *The Character of Ireland* will not appear other than as anecdotes of their travels, drinking and further requests, once back in England, for expenses to visit Ireland again. In the late '50s, Davin writes:

> If I would co-operate, with money, and let [Rodgers] have a session with Peadar O'Donnell. 'I'd get you the best stuff that ever was got

under the Irish lamps'.

This is Ireland as anthropological curio, a heart's desire and a great gas. It is the Ireland Rodgers tried to imagine in his poems too, under the contrary influences of MacNeice no doubt, but also of Dylan Thomas – not the wisest of artistic influences to follow. In the background, too, were the stricter and longer-lasting examples of 'the earlier English poets such as Herrick', who, according to Davin, Rodgers used in an effort to 'sidestep the rancorous antinomies of Ulster, and perhaps ... re-create a parochial idyll'. This is precisely what Rodgers sought to do, only to realise that the impossibility of any such project as *The Character of Ireland* also affected his own poetry. In 1963, a decade and more since the idea is first promulgated, Rodgers writes:

> Working on it both excites and depresses me, and I realise that to write about it is like opening an old wound, which is Ireland.

The following year, on another trip to Dublin for BBC recordings, Rodgers' comments are particularly revealing:

> Probably my reason in going [to Dublin] was to vivify my anger and love for the place and to find out why it was always so destructive to the likes of Louis and me. I think that I have found out part of the reason ... It wasn't an easy visit ... every day for five weeks I'd turn myself into a successful extrovert. I think I managed to do it, more equably than usual. But in the small hours of each morning my introverted mind, outraged, had to go mad. Yeats – Dev – Cosgrave etc – all the old timers – and all the old words I'd heard about them, would go berserk, come alive, and rampage through my brain with a will of their own but I managed to keep a hold, and to return to civilisation.

The long tortuous path of not writing *The Character of Ireland* lasted right up to his death in 1969, unfinished and unfinishable. There is, though, the extraordinary admission contained in the privacy of this letter of his acting out a role in Dublin ('turn myself'), the verbal energy with which he cannot cope ('the words go berserk') and the attempt to maintain control before 'the return to civilisation'.

This is a psychological state as much as an intellectual issue and it takes on imaginative implications as well because

Rodgers' own poetry embodies the conflict between all three points of this ideological tension. Rodgers tried to bluster it out with a generalised poetic rhetoric while simultaneously trying to create a kind of Edenic world wherein this conflict of interest would, quite simply, cease to exist.

In the second volume of his autobiography, *The Middle of My Journey* (1990), John Boyd recalls seeing W. R. Rodgers 'mount a pulpit and deliver a short sermon to a congregation of one – myself'.

> I cannot recall anything of what he said but he looked impressive standing slightly sideways as his usually soft voice resonated in the empty church. He loved words, perhaps he loved them too well, he was by nature a taciturn and diffident man who, when he was sober, used words sparingly, but when drunk he would scatter them so extravagantly that his hearers could hardly believe their ears.

There is about Rodgers the sense of melancholia, mixed with devilment and anxiety, which often characterises writers of his generation from a northern Protestant background. It was as if, located in London, but on frequent returns to Belfast, a cultural performance took place and this mask looked in various directions all at once. Whether in Dublin on BBC business, travelling through 'Ireland', in Belfast for a few days with old friends, before returning to London, or in London BBC haunts, there is something desperately self-conscious about MacNeice's and Rodger's sense of 'Irishness'. In lesser writers, this anxiety becomes professional, such as the embarrassing sight of northern Protestants faking 'Irish' accents and what they consider to be Irish mannerisms.

That Rodgers was 'a tortured and guilt-ridden man for most of his adult life', adds a truly tragic dimension to his artistic achievement. It is with the defining northern context of this achievement that Michael Longley begins his level-headed introduction to Rodgers' *Poems*:

> Ulster is still likely to produce poets who write out of a response to religion. Like his friend Louis MacNeice, Rodgers was motivated by strong anti-puritan feelings. The vividness they share was projected partly as an assault on religious narrowness and cultural restriction.

What influence these 'anti-puritan feelings' had on Rodgers' poetry is seen in his grasp of the difference between English and Irish poetry:

> ... the faculty of standing words or ideas on their heads – by means of pun, epigram, bull or what-have-you is a singularly Irish one. To the English ear, which likes understatement, it is all rather excessive and therefore not in good taste. But to the Irish mind, which likes gesture, bravado, gallivanting, and rhetoric, it is an acceptable tradition.

Whether or not such an 'acceptable tradition' actually exists is neither here nor there. The important thing is that Rodgers interpreted the 'Irish mind' in this, most romantic, way.

In very crude terms, the poetic side of Rodgers' nature warred with the social and cultural inheritance, while Minister Rodgers struggled to find a definite artistic identity as a poet. 'Ireland' became an imaginative home place or cultural alternative, ironically distanced from the London axis, of which Rodgers had become part, but separate, too, from the cramped provincialism of what he called the North, 'a backwater of literature out of sight of the running stream of contemporary verse'.

The poem is charged with resolving these tensions by revelling in 'a linguistic and rhythmic ebullience, a tendency to excess'. Yet, as Longley points out in his introduction, the weakest of Rodgers' poems are those which fall into this excess, becoming over-actively 'poetic' and 'Irish' with the 'O's, exclamation-marks and rhetoric anticipating the wilier textual play of Paul Muldoon:

> I am Ulster, my people an abrupt people
> Who like the spiky consonants in speech
> And think the soft ones cissy; who dig
> The k and t in orchestra, detect sin
> In sinfollia, get a kick out of
> Tin can, fricatives, fornication, staccato talk,
> Anything that gives or takes attack,
> Like Micks, Tagues, tinkers's gets, Vatican.

From 'Epilogue' to the never-completed *The Character of Ireland*, the poem ends with a rare mark of self-revelation:

And I, born to the purple passage,
Was heir to all that Adamnation
And hand-me-down of doom, the late comer
To the worn-out womb.
The apple blushed for me bellow Bellevue,
Lagan was my Jordan, Connswater
My washpot, and over Belfast
I cast out my shoe.

My own preference leads me to the shorter poems, such as 'Escape' rather than the operatic 'Europa and the Bull', 'Resurrection' or 'The Journey of the Magi'. As Longley points out, there is an erotic masterpiece in 'The Net' – its Elizabethan-like formality, edged with Auden, makes Rodgers a poet of real surprise and lasting joy:

Come, make no sound, my sweet;
Turn down the candid lamp
And draw the equal quilt
Over our naked guilt.

The chief characteristic of Rodgers' poetry retells a squabble with language in a fascinating early version of what has since become a major theme in Irish poetry: the self-consciousness of poets memorialising the language they write in. Voices, words, capitalised variations of both (like Humbug), mouths, silence, and galleries of abstractions like contempt, glory, imagination and pity are the stock in Rodgers' trade. He is finding a voice pitched somewhere between the parables and anecdotes of his scriptural life (as a Presbyterian minister) and a free form that verbally chastises the strictness he left behind him:

There, far from the slack noose of rumour
That tightens into choking fact, I relax.
And sound and sights and scents sail slowly by.
But suddenly, like delicate and tilted italics,
The upstanding birds stretch urgently away
Into the sky as suddenly grown grey.
Night rounds on Europe now. And I must go
Before its hostile faces peer and pour
Over the mind's rim enveloping me,
And my so-frightened thoughts dart here and there
Like trout among the grim stony gazes.

There is a great deal in Rodgers' poetry that has yet to be understood in the critical circles which determine the artistic and cultural value of a poet's work. In his writing, one senses how emblematic cultural options can take up a poet's time and get in the way of the real job which stares them in the face. Rodgers appreciated this dilemma and this is why there is the desire in his poetry for freedom, an awakening from which he, among others, could start again, as if from the beginning. Echoes of that yearning and rapture are found in the work of many writers and artists from a Protestant background. It is given fearsome poignancy in the revelations of Beckett, in the poetry of MacNeice and Longley, and in the music and lyrics of an artist Rodgers has probably the most in common with today, Van Morrison.

[1993]

# STRAY DOGS AND DARK HORSES:
## Seamus Heaney

Seamus Heaney's second book of criticism is much more personal than his first, *Preoccupations*. Behind the thematic design of *The Government of the Tongue*, there is a lot of searching for various influences and forces which the poet has to contend with in contemporary life. These forces are mostly cultural and literary but they have a powerful reality to them, as if they were of the same order as economics or politics.

*The Government of the Tongue* deals with sources of inspiration and artistic examples which gather round them: English, American and others. In a sense, it doesn't really matter where poets find inspiration, it's up to themselves. The interest is historical and makes for good reading when viewed as a tradition continuously being ventilated by new winds of change. The rhetorical undertow of these lectures and essays is the *perception* of change in contemporary literature in English:

> What translation has done over the last couple of decades is not only to introduce us to new literary traditions but also to link the new literary experience to a modern martyrology, a record of courage and sacrifice which elicits our unstinted admiration. So, subtly with a kind of hangdog intimation of desertion, poets in English have felt compelled to turn their gaze East and have been encouraged to concede that the locus of greatness is shifting away from their language.

Is there really such a reluctance to 'concede' literary value in other languages? If so, who are these poets who feel and think in this way? A few names and places might have given us something more to go on, but *The Government of the Tongue* is concerned with detecting trends and consequently its sweep is generously wide of any particular mark.

The parallel which Heaney establishes, for instance, with eastern European poets is interesting for the light it throws on his more recent poems, and is also provocative in terms of Irish poetry generally.

Despite Heaney's thoughtful and sensitive reading of eastern European poets, the question arises: is there not to be found in Italy or Spain a more apt connection with Ireland, with the cultural and moral dominance of an ultra-conservative church, a society politically divided by civil war, parochially partisan and conforming to populist images of itself? Perhaps a Pasolini or Lorca may have more to offer by way of artistic and critical analogy than a Mandelstam or Milosz. In terms of 'the North', with which *The Government of the Tongue* begins, are not imaginative contexts more readily available closer to home, in Scotland, for example, rather than in Zbigniew Herbert's Poland? For the problem of cultural identity in Scotland relates directly and historically to the conflict between political nationalism and religious patriotism on a scale more in keeping with our history than, say, the struggles of Poland.

The real distinctions emerge from the relationship between poet and state in eastern European and Soviet societies. Mandelstam or Akhmatova, Milocz or Herbert, relate 'oppositionally' to the cultural orthodoxies and beliefs of their countries. This cannot be said of contemporary Irish poets, because they are essentially insiders since little separates them from the cultural idealism of which their poetry and the historic Irish nation are assumed to be part, a point which many observers of contemporary Irish literature seem to ignore. Obviously this puts under such strain any analogy between eastern European and Irish poetry so that the only effective comparisons are the important imaginative ones: of style, diction, technique. Yet how do we work these out across the borders of languages which have so little in common? How close is eastern European poetry to ours in terms of content, or tone, or irony?

The individualistic intensity which Heaney portrays in his chapter on Sylvia Plath, and the barbarous knowledge which he sees Lowell tearing out of his own past are not customarily available in contemporary poetry, least of all in Ireland. This may well be the reason why Heaney writes on both poets: it is the attraction of opposites, since what characterises Heaney's poetry (and has made it so popular) is its inherently traditional manner. It is important to bear this in mind since, in many ways, these essays are against the grain of Modernism, even while they were written under the auspices of the T. S. Eliot Memorial Lectures.

The artistic challenge Heaney's work presents, like the intellectual patterning which *The Government of the Tongue* reveals, is notable for its comportment and balance: the moderate voice. One has the sense that Heaney knows exactly what he is doing here; this is not exploration or discovery but justification. Take the unassuming authority of the opening scene, for example; that it is significant in the first place establishes quite clearly Heaney's own faith in himself and his voice. The scene is a recording studio; there are constant reminders that the writer is a poet who deals with poetry (such as the opening gloss on 'The Impact of Translation'); these convey a slightly introverted quality, almost a sense of entrapment.

Yet the unshakeable rootedness forges links between poetry and politics (non-contentious), whereas the Ireland of 'one's origin' and the abstract reading of that place as literature has become contentiously thematic:

> The tongue, governed so long in the social sphere by tact and fidelity, by nice obeisances to one's origin with the minority or the majority, this tongue is suddenly ungoverned. It gains access to a condition that is unconstrained and, while not being practically effective, it is not necessarily inefficacious.

'... not necessarily inefficacious'? Is there any irony present? This decorum in *The Government of the Tongue* is troubling. However, the symmetry of Heaney's prose is always appealing. Sometimes Heaney goes overboard and his audience's expectations seem to nudge the pen a little too much. He talks of 'custardy vowels and gelinate consonants' in Lowell's *Day by Day* and stretches a metaphor that should be fairly suspect to begin with:

> Yet to enter a poetic career at this ultimate pitch was like Goldwyn's quest for the ultimate in movie excitement – something beginning with an earthquake and working up to a climax.

Heaney seems to be brooding on the moral state of poetry in the modern world but a real danger is that such brooding can take over:

> In the professionalised literary milieu of the west the poet is susceptible to self-deprecation and scepticism. The poet in the United States, for example, is aware that the machine of reputation-making and book distribution, whether it elevates or ignores him or her, is indifferent to the moral and ethical force of the poetry being distributed. A grant-aided pluralism of fashions and schools, a highly amplified language of praise which becomes the language of promotion and marketing, all this which produces from among the most gifted a procession of ironists and dandies and reflexive talents produces also a subliminal awareness of the alternative conditions and an anxious over-the-shoulder glance toward them.

So the west is a fallen Eden; the Garden remains in the east or in those peripheral places that speak a dialect of English, untouched or vindicated by their struggle against the imperium. Heaney's personal mythologising is important here, ('as I knelt like some latter-day croppy boy murmuring "Bless me, Father"...') but it is Patrick Kavanagh who proves the talisman:

> Whether he wanted it or not, [Kavanagh's] achievement was inevitably co-opted, North and south, into the general current of feeling which flowed from and sustained ideas of national identity, cultural otherness from Britain and the dream of a literature with a manner and a matter resistant to the central Englishness of the dominant tradition.

It is a perfectly laudable 'dream', yet deeply ironic that to accomplish it ordinarily means the acceptance of those channels of 'the professionalized literary milieu in London and the States' which are otherwise to be resisted. (Although the example of modernists like Beckett, Coffey or Devlin casts a different perspective here). In this respect, *The Government of the Tongue* is an intellectual constituency; literally, a region of the mind. This confirms the sense of Heaney the poet as being, strictly speaking, an unpolitical poet, interested more in poetic ideas. While these ideas may have political implications, the main drift of Heaney's imagination is intellectual.

It would have been interesting, for instance, to read Heaney on 'a certain partisan strain in the criticism of Irish Poetry' which he associates with Anthony Cronin, but he demurs – 'worth taking up in another context'. By contrast, discussing the 'urban world', Iain Crichton Smith, the Scottish poet, in *Towards the Human: Selected Essays* (1986), remarks:

> ... it is quite possible that the contradictions in society itself are so deep that it may not be able to supply its own people with the necessities of life. Nor will anyone be satisfied with the impression of sordidness ... travelling through British cities, the breakdown of transport, the graffiti which shows the aggression of the 'homeless', the language of hatred, ferocious and mis-spelt, the feeling that one has of an urban world breaking down: the rushing from late trains to vandalised telephones, as if this was a land where people no longer feel at home. Such a world is not progress, it is the sick turning-back of progress itself, for the uprooted are taking on society by turning against it and writing on walls the grotesque language which is the reality that lies deeply beneath the contradictions of schools and other institutions. Where is the home of the urban dweller now? And if he looks into his mind what does he see but images of aggression and violence, beggary and greed, hatred and envy? ... It is against such a failure that one can set the idea of community, the idea of a culture ...

What *The Government of the Tongue* is dealing with on a formal level is the reconciliation of the poet's place between 'the idea of community' and 'the idea of a culture'. The social base of this mediation has, however, been evacuated. Yet, like all that Seamus Heaney has written and said, what shines through is a love of literature, of the Word and of being in the world. His presence is wholly affirmative. This is what makes his work as a poet and critic so important and necessary. As Heaney says himself:

> The fact is that poetry is its own reality and no matter how much a poet may concede to the corrective pressures of social, moral, political

and historical reality, the ultimate fidelity must be to the demands and promise of the artistic event.

That said, there is nevertheless every good reason for poets in this day and age to bury their heads in the critical sands, so treacherously immediate has the making of reputations become. Going by the sheer volume of work devoted to the poetry and critical prose of Seamus Heaney, it is nothing short of a miracle that he has not stepped through the looking-glass and disappeared. For Heaney, the Nobel Laureate, has turned into even more of an icon now than he was in the late 1970s and 80s.

His writing is scrutinised and mountains made out of molehills, without any real understanding coming through in regard to what Heaney is as a poet. This is a fate worse than neglect but Heaney, to his infinite credit, has managed to keep ahead of the posse. Indeed, there seems little sign of his losing interest in the argy-bargy of being, in the fading embers of this century, the most discussed poet writing in English.

I have not seen Heaney's poetry as anything near as intellectually demanding, artistically labyrinthine or morally coquettish as many critics self-approvingly maintain. The conclusive anthropological surge of Heaney's earlier books such as *Death of a Naturalist* (1966) and *Door into the Dark* (1969), matched by their nostalgic playfulness, made his poetry immediately amenable to popular taste. It was justly celebrated by that fact alone. In *Wintering Out* (1972) and *North* (1975) Heaney raised the stakes by mythologising the landscapes and history of his homeland before the impeccable *Field Work* (1979) brought him to a cooler, sharper and more personal grace.

The big change that came about in *Station Island* (1984) and *The Haw Lantern* (1987) was two-fold. There was an impatient breaking out towards something intellectually worked-at and considered as the old consolation of language was worried over. The consciousness of his audience also seemed to press in and around the poems. Heaney the poet became increasingly more visible and profiled in the poetry until, in *Seeing Things* (1991) he constructed a return to his family's collective past.

Heaney has been fortunate in being able, through dint of his own personality and the breadth of his appeal, to keep his work within reach of the common reader while simultaneously not alienating the critics. He writes for that middle ground and has respected it and given it back respect at a very difficult time. During his rise to international recognition throughout the 70s and early 80s, the language of criticism became increasingly more specialist. While preoccupied with cultural studies, there was also much critical talk about accessibility and popular arts. Heaney's poetry bridged the gap by being both literary and available. It is an extraordinary balancing act.

However, Heaney's writing has started to receive the cooling attentions of, among others, feminist critics. It is embroiled in the post-colonial debate. All of which has nothing, of course, to do with Heaney himself. It has, however, quite a lot to do with where he came from and what he has made of it in his own poetry and prose. While 'English' and the 'Empire' reeled from the ceaseless assault of vernacularism – local speech, folklore, the cultural rights of previously unarticulated social experience – the literal centre no longer held sway.

Poets of the imagined marshes took over the Tower. So the idea that literature was itself a battlefield proved fatally attractive and the decade of political correctness (the 1980s) opened out in the United States with the possibility of poets, critics and intellectuals engaging in what was necessary and central. To get near the really bloody, historically messy territories such as the North's deluded war of independence was to the critical-media generation of the 1980s what Spain proved to be in the 1930s. (Hands up those who remember El Salvador?)

When Seamus Heaney, a richly nuanced and confident voice from the last dominion, won prominence inside the Pale, his work would be read as representing Ireland, indeed, as being Ireland. Yet as the wizardly W. H. Auden put it: 'Every poet is at once a representative of his culture and its critic'; Heaney has fulfilled one side of the aphorism, but not the other. Whatever unease he may or may not feel about the Ireland we live in does not surface in his poetry. There is an acceptance of this place as it is which ranges from the stoical to the faithful.

Beyond such notions of cultural allegiance and understanding, Heaney represents something perhaps more powerful in the eyes of that wider English-speaking culture in which he was schooled. If the real politics of power, class struggle and issues of authority and social control were eclipsed by the universal monetarist meanness of the 1980s, what rose from the depths was an intellectual anxiety about the value of art and its ability to salvage some sense of civic influence and cultural counter-weight. Heaney's presence embodies such gravitas as much as his art consoles.

For when it appears throughout the English-speaking world that all the cultural co-ordinates of the 'established' political and moral code have collapsed, Heaney's poetry can be read as harbinger of a postmodernist future as well as keeper of the traditional virtues. No small wonder then that critics, across the Irish Sea and, more importantly, across the Atlantic, respond most positively to a writer who attempts to redress this widening gulf with work that is linked to the general crisis and to the general public.

Against this, though, there are the debatable terms of critical reference by which contemporary poetry is read. And, unfortunately, quite a lot of what has been written about Seamus Heaney's work is colourless and agenda-driven. As Patricia Craig remarked, the enemy of the day is earnestness. But there is also the unctuous gravity and slick processing within which all contemporary poetry is shredded.

Barbara Everett, in her collection of essays, *Poets in Their Time* (1986), has suggested that current critical practices overstress:

> ... the side of poetry concerned with communication of statements ... and understress the side which is more private, less communicative perpetuation of experience, deriving as much from a universe of things, as from a language of concepts. They do this unavoidably,

because they are philosophical terms abstracted from discourse, and discourse is fully public as poetry is not; to debate about poetry at all is partly to falsify what often takes its strength from inarticulated intelligence; and it is from these necessary falsifications that there proceed the endless and equally necessary in-fightings of criticism.

The quality of this public discourse has rarely been taken into critical consideration but what seems certain is that a poet like Heaney has become a figure in a cultural war-of-words not of his own making in the midst of much vicarious anger on behalf of the People, it was only to be expected that when a poet such as Heaney won prominence inside the Pale, his work would be read as radical. Similarly, those who started to see their roles as ideological as much as literary began a process of re-examination during the 1980s which is now beginning to bear fruit.

For these writers, along with many other women poets, black poets, gay and lesbian writers, all with specific issues in mind, and deftly managing the professionalisation of the arts (or its Americanisation) now make up the dominant and key players in a very real multi-cultural crisis that is taking place at the heart of the English-speaking world. Northern Ireland, if you like, is no longer culturally special and, placed in the wider context of Europe, is fast becoming yesterday's news.

The 'inarticulated intelligence' of poetry is facing, in other words, a lean time, and expectations are placed squarely on 'public discourse' as a congregation of particular themes, poetic attitudes and political issues.

In a sense, Heaney's poetry is illuminated by the crossfire. Henry Hart's well-researched *Seamus Heaney: Poet of Contrary Progressions* takes a fairly schematic approach to its ultimate pitch by literally accepting at face-value literary influences and comparisons:

> ... when elegy fails to deliver satisfactory consolation revenge tragedy intervenes to fill the vacuum (and it is interesting to note that at Queen's University 'the dramatic poetry of [Christopher] Marlowe and [John] Webster appealed' greatly to Heaney.

We read that Heaney's move to Glanmore in 1972 was

'controversial – for whom, where and why? – while bearing with Hart offers critical insight, the struggle is often with his writing style:

> The moral value of this poetry that vigilantly investigates cultural dilemmas but then dissolves its solutions and that deconstructs the ancient hierarchies and oedipal struggles between 'patriarchal' British Protestants and 'matriarchal' Irish Catholics bothers Heaney because it fails to articulate concrete political resolutions for Ireland.

The assumption of eloquent reason in this anti-climax (*bothers?*) should put the reader on guard against some dodgy critical drift. 'Heaney's former status' we are told 'as a 'non-citizen' in Protestant-dominated Northern Ireland derived at least in part from his decision to choose writing as his mode of expression rather than the more customary political organ, speech.' This critspeak finally becomes exasperating as the real political 'non-citizens' of the North – the dead, maimed and imprisoned – drop out of sight in a burst of, albeit well-meaning, literary rhetoric.

Michael Parker's *Seamus Heaney: The Making of the Poet* is a much wiser, less ambitious and more knowledgeable book. Almost to the point of adulation, his study is an impressionistic account of Heaney's artistic and professional development, ready-made for the general reader and student alike. What makes Parker's book recommendable is the author's lucid meshing of the poems with their immediate cultural and political contexts, rather than using these solely as ideological counters.

The terms of Elmer Andrews' *Seamus Heaney: A Collection of Essays* range from the wider picture of Maurice Harmon's 'We Pine for Ceremony: Ritual and Reality in the Poetry of Seamus Heaney, 1965–75' to the button-holing manner of James Simmons in 'The Trouble with Seamus'.

Characteristically careful and insightful essays by Andrews, Terence Brown, Robert Welch (with a particularly fine essay on poetic freedom in Heaney), Michael Allen and John Lucas rub shoulders with 'Pap for the Dispossessed: Seamus Heaney and the Poetics of Identity' by David Lloyd.

This essay, subsequently reprinted in Lloyd's *Anomalous States: Irish Writing and the Post-Colonial Moment* (1993), is a good example of the extenuating priorities of the current critical climate. The spiderish prose-style should not, however, be discounted, because there is a sting in the tale as Heaney is cut down to the status of 'minor poet' at the behest of the following categorical imperatives:

> Even insurgent or anti-colonial violence, generally speaking directed against the state apparatus, can become in the strict sense 'terrorist' where it seeks by symbolic rather than tactical acts to force integration or identity within the discursive boundaries already established and maintained by dominant hegemony. A socialist or feminist critique of such tendencies has to be located not in a generalised criticism of 'men of violence', but in the analysis of the totalising effect of an identity thinking that discretely links terrorism to the state in whose name it is condemned. For what is at stake is not so much the practice of violence, which has long been institutionalised in the bourgeois state, as its aestheticisation in the name of a freedom expressed in terms of national or racial integration. This aesthetic frame deflects attention from the interests of domination which the national state expresses both as idea and as entity.

During the late '50s and early '60s there was much made of 'The Death of the Novel'. The 90s may well prove to be 'The Crux for Criticism'. High visibility poets such as Seamus Heaney will, however, keep on writing, fuelling debate of one kind or another. There will also always be the stray dogs and dark horses, snuffling in the high grass, doing very much their own impractical thing. We should be mindful and judicious in understanding that what separates all their work from the law and order of literary politics is the real point. In Lloyd's fascinating revisioning of Irish writers (Yeats, Beckett and Heaney, amongst others) there is a powerful argument gathering force which will radically shift the way poets are read under the now dominant critical dispensation.

[1987–1992]

# A GRITTY PROD BAROQUE: Tom Paulin

From the opening poem, 'Under Creon', Tom Paulin's *The Liberty Tree* (1983) is an argument about history, its victims and the unburied issues of the past which continue to haunt our present. It is an argument about justice and blame that Paulin has been conducting since his first book, *A State of Justice*, was published in 1977, followed in 1980 by *The Strange Museum*. Both books were well received, particularly in England. Here was a poet, English-born but brought up in Belfast, educated there and in England, who offered a new perspective on Ireland. For a start, he was a Protestant and, as the poems showed, he was involved in the urban world, not the rural.

Paulin's poetry has, too, an intellectual sharpness – some might say, stringency – that is refreshing; his style has an Orwellian sense of suburban decay many critics find appealing. His poetry also fits a traditional English bill, but updated by a thoughtful integration within it of the modernist ethic of Mandelstam's poetry and of the figure of Mandelstam himself as symbolic of the Poet in the real Twentieth Century.

Comparison with Seamus Heaney's work is obvious on this level but, whereas Heaney delves down deep into the tangled roots of language, Paulin transplants them on to the construction site of history. His use of language is contractual, civic-minded, keeping his distance from the hot house of what Heaney called 'Our tribe's complicity'. In a sense, Paulin, the Protestant, cannot commit himself to the absurd, doomed, guilt-ridden 'Protestant' cause to stem what Heaney called, in 'At the Water's Edge', the 'scared, irrevocable steps' of the just Catholic march of history. To be able to speak with such confidence clearly bolsters a poet's self-image. Being denied this complicity, the poet sees his landscape and language as somewhat irredeemable, marred by an oppressiveness of its own making; the poet speaks, therefore, of the seedy irrelevance of lower middle-class Protestantism in the last throes of its political hegemony and power.

Paulin's poetry holds itself off from delving into the material and psychic chaos of this background. His language is forced to make such contact neutral, observant, pointedly unengaged. The words themselves are adjectivally abstract, forming around the places and ideas of his poetry a bleak impressionism. Indeed, one picks at random words and phrases – 'stillness', 'forgiveness', 'politeness', 'blueness', 'greyness', 'graceless', 'worthless', 'dullness', 'colourless', 'whiteness', 'paleness', 'nameless', 'gentleness', 'bitterness', 'darkness', 'sadness', 'clearness', 'grey tenderness', 'banal sickness', 'banal stale atmosphere', 'taut dryness' – to illustrate Paulin's dependency upon stock poeticisms while the supply of his ideas is carried by the declamatory titles, narratives and restrained confessions in an other's voice.

If *The Strange Museum* was marked by Paulin's over-emphasis, the kind of split-level in which each poem dwelt, formally portraying scenes of similar proportion while the ideological theme-work went on down below, *The Liberty Tree* bends under the weight of its own ambitious language. For it seeks to collapse the distinction, philosophical as much as poetic, between 'a dead light in the room' and where this leads to in *The Strange Museum*, 'the long lulled pause/Before history happens'. Pervasive moments of apprehension characterise the earlier volumes. In *The Liberty Tree*, however, Paulin tries to weld together, in the very language he uses, the perceiving figure and scene of his poems with that which rules them – history. He is, in other words, not interested in stillnesses or pauses, but in a language that protests its own materiality, its perverse embroilment in history. For all the questioning of the earlier volumes, Paulin has found what I can only call a 'mock realism'; it is a change from historic Time to verbal Space and it takes him out of the picture.

*The Liberty Tree* does not record speech, though; the poems are attempts to speak in 'the people's voice'. How does this show itself in the book? Again, at random, one comes up against words, phrases and, what seems to me, caricature, which keeps the poetry on a very literary axis of being. These range from colloquialisms to a peculiar jargon I cannot quite place but which reminds me of the schoolboy comics and Christmas annuals which told tales of imperial might in the idiom of Kipling.

I list those which strike me as being most illustrative of Paulin's lexicon. A 'scuffy sort of place', where scuff means to drag your feet, thus damaging shoes; 'the biffy road', where biff is a thump in children's parlance, although I cannot make the connection with road; 'flups'; 'a farty hardboard hut' meaning small and useless. All which come from 'Exogamy'.

In 'Descendancy', Paulin remarks that 'All those family histories/are like sucking a polo mint' and completes the analogy with, 'you're pulled right through/a tight wee sphincter/that loses you'. The sense of the unselfconscious 'tight wee' drawn up beside the technical 'sphincter' is a deliberate act of Paulin's but I am unsure why: to domesticate 'sphincter' or to legitimise 'tight wee' and the community the phrase comes from? However one sees it, the object of 'Descendancy' gets reduced to a squabble over words that wrestle with each other as the meaning remains hidden in terms of specific conflict: 'Could be that a third one/ – say an ex-B Special – /has pulled up at a road block/a shade far from Garrison?' This enigma stays as an enigma and the poem is validated extraneously by the factor of the present politico-cultural climate working in the poet's favour to explicate the matter.

One moves on to 'After the Summit' in which the first stanza opens with a peculiarly Belfast phrase, 'wee buns', meaning easily done, and proceeds into other colloquialisms like 'the boul Jimmy, your man Craig' and 'a dacent ould skin'. The comprehending narrator of the second stanza recounts, like a voice-over, 'There is so little history/we must remember who we are'. But from the appropriated vitality of the language in the first stanza to the solemnity of the second, we really get little choice in making our own minds up as to what is actually going on in the poem. Its frame of reference is sealed shut with that dogmatic and far from self-justifying conclusion which preaches to us.

Who is the 'we', for instance? It refers to the Protestants of Northern Ireland, as poems like 'Desertmartin' and 'Descendancy' testify. Yet, time and again, I am forced back to the devices Paulin uses to depict their reality. Consider, for example, the second stanza of 'Politik':

> I'd be dead chuffed if I could catch
> the dialects of those sea-loughs,
> but I'm scared of all that's hard
> and completely subjective.

The vernacular *dead chuffed* rises out of the poem in brash self-consciousness, but then its very essence in the poem is challenged by the poet's wish to do what he has actually achieved – to use from 'the dialects' one term of reference 'dead chuffed'. So it is confusing to confess that he is scared of that world while, simultaneously, making deliberate use of parts of its language. The poet really cannot have it both ways. Only out of the control of the 'completely subjective' can any true grasp of a people's language and, consequently their experience, emerge. This involves sympathy, an artistic enterprise of conflicting proportion which may well lead, ironically, into a radically formal diction, rather than the highly formalised unliterary one which Paulin has created in *The Liberty Tree*.

I do not sense, either, the necessary complication of feeling in this book. Paulin seems to have his mind made up but the emotional range of the poetry is unexplored. Take 'Politik' again:

> ... those quartzy voices in the playground
> of a school called Rosetta Primary
> whose basalt and sandstone have gone
> like Napoleon into Egypt ...

The reader is left literally bereft, not knowing what to think because Paulin does not present himself in the poem to take responsibility for what he is actually feeling and saying. Instead, he is there to make the necessary connections, the expert monitoring on his 'carbon-dater' the abstract lives of shadowy people. But, since *The Liberty Tree* deals so explicitly with 'a plain Presbyterian grace', we must expect something more than metaphorical ambiguities. This bothers me for two reasons: firstly, because the images of *The Liberty Tree* will probably be accepted without much thought given to what they effectively say about the Protestant people of Northern Ireland; secondly, because I admire Paulin as a poet and feel that *The Liberty Tree* represents only a truncated flowering of his art.

My dispute with this book is over what I perceive to be a continuing resistance in Paulin's work to release, imaginatively, feelings and beliefs of a much more personal nature, engendered in the complex individual experience and the formative influence of being – or seeing oneself as being – a northern Protestant.

Out of the pores of that body politic must come the privatised guilts, fears and hopes of men and women who symbolise, in all their bewildering, and widely perceived, ungracious belligerence, the modern state of homelessness. They represent, as William Faulkner's characters represent, the need to conquer an onerous fate and to reconstruct a sense of community outside themselves – tasks of a truly historic kind. This is not, I trust, the language of a false apocalypse and I certainly do not intend to use it as a spectacular rule against which to measure the imaginative accomplishment of *The Liberty Tree*. But these tasks, or imaginative responsibilities, do order the emotional and social framework I bring to bear upon *The Liberty Tree* and they make all the more forceful my impressions of how this book undermines what are its own real achievements. I see this most clearly in 'Off the Back of a Lorry', a short piece of twenty-one lines. The language moves from a laid-back detective-story jargon of 'two rednecks troughing/ in a gleaming diner' to Paisley 'putting pen to paper in Crumlin jail'. The images are cinematic and, whatever associations we make with them, they coalesce in the poet's own stating of them as 'pured fictions'. The poem then turns accusingly:

> ... and like the small ads
> in a country paper
> they build a gritty
> sort of prod baroque
> I must return to
> like my own boke.

This poem depresses me because it is a dead-end and reflects in a totally negative way upon Paulin's real ability as a poet. It is, frankly, a biased piece of demotic writing. As a poem, it hardly gets a chance to get on its feet. The stills by which it develops are black and white and so they end up illuminating little other than the poet's seeming contempt for what he is writing about. I would question again the use of language: the vernacular 'prod' for Protestant camouflages the flippant exuberance of 'baroque', unless, eccentrically, the poet means through 'gritty' the original French of 'mis-shapen pearl' and, if so, where does that leave us – the unlikely action of the poet going back to his own 'boke' (vomit)?

The faltering of nerve, or the pressures of other influences, have unsettled Paulin's artistic poise in too many of the poems of *The Liberty Tree*. This unbalances the book, eclipsing such fine poems as 'Black Bread' and 'The Book of Juniper' by forcing arguments rather than revealing Paulin's artistic reasoning. Broaching the dangers of unfashionable complicities will create a richly human art out of Paulin's quarrel with the past. To call on Yeats, as a last resort, it might be no harm for Paulin to quarrel a little bit more fervently with himself.

## II

Sometimes I have this ridiculous dream. I am at a party twenty years from now. There is a woman talking at me in one of those

Cherry Valley accents (the Belfast equivalent of Dublin's apocryphal DARTspeak) and she's telling me earnestly how many generations of her Protestant people have lived on this island and that she has just discovered Irish literature and that the other day too she bought a bodhrán for her husband. Meanwhile, over in the corner, a friend is patiently negotiating a debate he has had a million times before about the survival of the Irish language. By this time most of Belfast has dual-signposts, street-names and learning classes have sprung up in several community colleges in the better-off districts and also in a few of the twilight zones: so-called because Protestants and Catholics are still occasionally beaten-up in these grey areas banking on to the new ghettos – rambling, grass-verged estates bristling with an explosive, unverifiable pride and embittered rage.

I nod my head and accept her new-found enthusiasm but see out of the window beyond her, over the castellated view of roof and chimney-top, a part of the city where I grew up. It is all changed by now but it has kept a grand prospect over the lough. This is a world that does not exist but it probably will – one day.

A different state of ambiguity exists in Paulin's *Ireland and the English Crisis* (1984), a collection of essays and reviews revolving around literature and politics:

> My own critical position is eclectic and is founded on an idea of an identity which has as yet no formal or institutional existence.

Paulin's state is a peculiarly personal one that sounds political and has the aura about it ('as yet') of historical necessity. He finds himself 'drawn to John Hume's eloquence, his humane and constitutional politics' and rebuking 'provincialism' (that tawny old hare), feels no longer 'either in Ireland or England, any hostility towards a southern insouciance'.

I am not sure what this 'insouciance' means – 'that ironical manner ... so characteristic of Dublin culture' of page 24 or, perhaps, 'the deep hostility which much of that community [in the south] feels towards both communities in the North' of page 25? Either way, Paulin's no longer feeling hostile to 'it' is of some note since he relates both to the 'Ireland' and the 'English crisis' of his title. Precisely how these link up is not explored but stated:

> In moments of aggravation it seems to me that if England no longer wants both the canon of English literature and the desperate, wrecked state of Northern Ireland, then perhaps something could be created out of this double rejection?

The connection rests upon an even more tenuous relatedness than these 'moments of aggravation'. In his introduction, from which the two main quotations above are taken, Paulin refers to 'Once a full Irish identity has been established then some form of sceptical detachment ... becomes necessary and obligatory'.

I would have thought it 'necessary and obligatory' for writers to stick to the truth that they know and that this obligation is paramount, 'sceptical detachment' or no. It certainly is not welded programmatically to 'a full Irish identity' as if the latter was something one constructed out of cultural Lego, like 'a full Irish breakfast'.

Like people, the imagination is not logical; it is often drawn to what repels it. 'Then' does not necessarily exist – it depends upon what people think, feel, experience and how they interpret this. And a writer cannot surely post-date his own experience or lock parts of it away until some possible state of grace or some political 'solution' designates the establishment of 'a full Irish identity'. I was surprised, too, that Paulin did not take this opportunity to examine his own assertion: 'the recognition that the Irish writer who publishes in Britain has a neo-colonial identity. And the central question which faces the neo-colonial writers is – whom am I writing for?'

Is it that transparently obvious – for what about the audience to whom such a question is itself pitched? And there are other questions which hardly ruffle the sleeve of *Ireland and the English Crisis*. Paulin writes, again in the introduction, that:

> ... most Unionists have a highly selective memory and cling
> desperately to a raft constructed from two dates – 1690 and 1912.
> The result is an unusually fragmented culture and a snarl of
> superficial or negative attitudes. A provincialism of the most disabling
> kind.

But Paulin's reluctance to distinguish between 'Unionism'
and the complex reasons why ordinary people in the North of
Ireland feel themselves to be 'British' rather than 'Irish' is a
crucial oversight. Calling it 'that mythic consumer durable'
(feeling British, not Irish) does not really get us far in
understanding why so many people in the North want to stay
'British' while, before their very eyes, their homes, factories,
and that elusive 'way of life', corrodes into a brittle and
unsustainable formalism.

There is, though, nothing 'unusually fragmented' about the
Ulster Protestant Culture, its 'selectivity' is common enough in
these islands and the 'snarl' a conventional target easily
transferable to other locations. I can still see, for instance, the
bloodlessly ecstatic face of an Irish journalist at some literary
reception being stuck into my own with the self-satisfied
words: Doesn't your own lot usually kill their traitors!

Paulin hits the point with 'disabling', but its context is
dismissive and neglects the sympathetic justice of criticism such
as one finds in Sarah Nelson's *Ulster's Uncertain Defenders:
Loyalists and the Northern Ireland Conflict* (1984). Indeed, the
entire thrust of *Ireland and the English Crisis* abandons the
present condition and history of such people (the million or so)
in favour of raising literary questions about being an Irish
writer 'with his neo-colonial identity'. I would have thought
the other matter much more pressing, if less popular, as the war
in the North drags relentlessly on, claiming the lives of young
men and women and making the conventional sense of
'Ireland' as a historical community into a very sick joke.

Paulin is right in much of what he says in this book,
particularly in his treatment of contemporary England. And it
is nice to 'assume the existence of a non-sectarian, republican
state which comprises the whole island of Ireland'. In Ireland,

many assume it every day and fight for it in many different and, often, costly ways: women's health issues, sheltering the poor and homeless, protecting the rights of minorities, restoring to a fuller life those suffering from drug and alcohol abuse, resisting the decay of rural towns and villages, coping with emigration and battling for the civil and social rights of the unemployed. But it would be naive to assume that the major block to the establishment 'of a non-sectarian republican state' comes solely from the Unionists or the grim reapers in the British state. The political and religious power-structures in the present Republic and its exclusivist social legislation are as determinedly against such a non-sectarian 'republican' state in practice as were the miserable and bigoted policies of the ex-governing party in the North.

Along with Paulin, most sensible people wish to see the neighbouring country across the water 'fully multi-racial, nuclear-free and more socially just'. But, again, in the world where we actually live it is not simply a matter of choice, even with such a harmless option as this one. And we are only kidding ourselves (and fooling no one else) if we think it can be any different for a writer, including those whom Paulin discusses in *Ireland and the English Crisis* – Joyce, Yeats, MacNeice, Auden and Kavanagh. Paulin brings this shifting contradiction fully into focus. There is the occasional editorial infelicity, as with the contradictory statements on pages 127 and 128 about 'moles' and the Northern Ireland Civil Service. There may be too many short pieces but with excellent articles like 'The Making of a Loyalist', 'National Myths', 'The Writer Underground', 'English Now' and 'Paisley's Progress', *Ireland and the English Crisis* is an invaluable and pioneering step taken by an Irish poet into the minefield of literary and social criticism.

### III

In his *Faber Book of Political Verse* (1986), however, Paulin labours under the strain of much literary self-consciousness.

Possibly as a result of the state of literary affairs in England (which he charted in *Ireland and the English Crisis*), Paulin's anthology is a personal selection of poems that can be only roughly categorised as 'political'.

The introduction is full of imperatives ('must' is commonplace) and condemnation, implied or overt – Hopkins' head rolls, for instance, 'as a right-wing patriot'. Links are forged by the new time, traditions established, influences traced and unspecified factors abound, like the 'certain intent cadence' of Yeats or his 'more brutal qualities', as well as 'certain imaginative positives in Heaney' or 'certain schools of literary criticism'. One yearns for specifics.

Editorial static is earthed, however, by standard literary complaints:

> In the Western democracies it is still possible for many readers, students and teachers of literature to share the view that poems exist in a timeless vacuum or a soundproof museum, and that poets are gifted with an ability to hold themselves above history, rather like skylarks or weather satellites.

Is this really true of the vast bulk of schools and colleges throughout Europe, Britain or Ireland – even of those which think structuralism has something to do with architecture? I would have thought that, in the majority of these places, the poet is viewed as a writer of processable footnotes to historical events, personal scenes from life, or as a painter of definable landscapes: all very much giving up students to boredom and the fidgets as poems are learnt as facts, but not of poets being 'timeless' or 'above history'. This is a problem 'the Poet' encounters far more than the reader.

In contrast to this, there is 'the ironic gravity and absence of hope in poets such as Herbert, Rozewicz, Holub [which] reminds us that in Eastern Europe the poet has a responsibility both to art and to society, and that this responsibility is single and indivisible'.

I would not quibble with this but, rather, with the over-determination of categories and tradition-making which Paulin goes in for in his introduction. A poet like Elizabeth Bishop is squeezed into place as 'patrician' and as 'a social critic' whose 'sophisticated quietism' makes her 'a silent political poet', in spite of herself! It is a lack of discretion to assume the mantle of speaking on behalf of 'we in the west' as a people 'who have difficulty in comprehending' the plight of fellow human beings in the east, and that 'we ... too readily twist to our own smug purposes' the message these poets send. But who is this 'we'?

Moving from the introduction, the selection of poems is quixotic. One wonders about the predominant influence of the Irish contingent, in comparison with the relatively small presence of those established 'political' European poets saluted in the introduction. A poem apiece from Brecht, Enzensberger and Holub, but five poems from Seamus Heaney, three from Derek Mahon, two from Paul Muldoon and contributions from a motley crew of Egan O'Rahilly, Fear Dorcha Ó Meállain, Swift, Joyce, Yeats, Longley and Deane. Pablo Neruda pips it with one poem, as does Pasternak; while Anna Akhmatova's single poem is one of the six translations contributed by the editor. Tony Harrison – the most political poet writing in England today – has one poem which keeps him in the company of Berryman, Bishop, Eliot, Frost, Hill, Hughes, Lawrence and Owen.

On the other hand, poets like Jeffrey Wainwright and Christopher Middleton do not feature at all. Nor do any of the 'political' poets like Padraic Fiacc, John Montague, Brendan Kennelly, Paul Durcan or James Simmons, while neither 'Nightwalker' nor 'Butcher's Dozen' by Thomas Kinsella get a look in.

The selections are perplexing. Perhaps Dryden's *Absalom and Achitophel* is 'a great masterpiece' but trying to convince teachers and students that it does not 'exist in a soundproof museum' is another day's work. In any case, John Cooper Clarke's fashionable hype of 'the fucking days are fucking long' is not a masterpiece.

Whether or not 'a popular verse tradition' appears to be extinct in England may prove a rum point in 'certain circles' but, given the absence of contemporary Irish ballads and songs,

Paulin has missed the chance to include popular works like 'The Men Behind the Wire', 'Take Me Home to Mayo' or 'The Ballad of Bobby Sands'. One is left with Paulin's declared 'hope' that this book will 'contribute towards the creation of a broad "canon" of political verse in English'. If the 'polemical' introduction, which, the Preface says, Craig Raine ('who commissioned the anthology') 'provoked', had been shortened from its 37 pages, more space might have been found for poems rather than for the call to arms of 'canon-fodder'.

## IV

If *The Faber Book of Political Verse* is marred by a missionary self-consciousness, Paulin's fourth volume of poems, *Fivemiletown* (1987), carries a similar burden. Before turning to the poems, however, it might be useful to take a look at the assumptions which surround the book. This is what is written on its back-cover:

> [Paulin] continues his exploration of the Northern Irish predicament, but at an even higher pitch of risk than he attempted before. The theme of Protestant identity is considered in both local and global terms, and Paulin's devices, which here range from the most measured and laconic statements, to utterances that threaten to defy all formal constraints, demonstrate the radical nature of his response to a major cultural crisis. *Fivemiletown* is an astonishing and explosive performance.

The 'higher pitch of risk' should put the reader on guard, because writing poetry in these islands rarely involves personal risk, only the possibility of artistic failure. As in the past, Paulin has not been well served by his blurb-writers. Here, one jibs at such clarion-calls as 'utterances that threaten to defy all formal constraints' – which sounds like a blood-vessel about to burst – while the 'radical nature' of Paulin's 'response to a major cultural crisis' begs more questions than one book of poetry can ever hope to answer and, maybe, should ever try. What does *radical* mean in this context – using short lines and what used to be called 'bad language'? A radical poet is surely someone, like Brian Coffey, who recasts the entire nature of poetic language. And which particular 'major cultural crisis' is being referred to here – the break-up of Britain? The disfigured face of violence in the North? These things are not disclosed by *Fivemiletown*.

Having read and re-read the book, I am not sure either what it has to do with the declared 'theme' of Protestant identity considered in 'both local and global terms'. Since when were poets supposed to state their themes, anyway, outside the seminar room? And the 'Northern Irish predicament': *predicament*?

Following *The Liberty Tree*, Paulin has continued writing 'dialect poems'. These are not just taken from his perceptions of how English is spoken in the North but, also, from how it is spoken in England by intellectuals who read poetry and write about it. There are, for example, a lot of words italicised in *Fivemiletown*. This denotes meaning over and above the poem's own proven significance. Words like *sdark*, *sput*, *whap* and others. Foreign phrases are liberally scattered through the book as well: 'mon cabinetnoir', 'Kurbishutte', 'Schwarzerd' and 'differance'. There also continues to be a sub-text of literary chat about speech, the demotic, reading and the declaration, in one of the poems from and about writers:

– I'm letting you off the hook, Albion,
not for your own sake, never,
but because out of your steam presses
shot Dickens, Darwin, Spencer and Mill!

What differentiates *Fivemiletown* from previous collections is the vigorous use of four-letter words and sexuality. There are lots of 'fucks', 'fucking', 'a drunken fuck', school-girl knickers, bums, funky vulvas, breasts, quick blow-jobs. In 'Really Naff', we read:

I notched his neck with my lips.
In bed he was all thumbs –
I was jabbed like a doorbell –
until he collapsed
sticky with the promise
of making my bum.

while 'Brez Marine' has the following:

> and that night in bed
> I stuck my winedark tongue
> inside her bum
> her blackhaired Irish bum

The 'higher pitch of risk' mentioned on the jacket by any chance?

We also read of 'the operation/on the Dauphin's foreskin', 'left testicles' crop up in the same poem, while in a half-dozen poems or so Paulin returns rather mechanically to sex and sexual encounters. Whether doing 'it best/in the bath' or 'meeting in this room/with no clothes on – to believe in nothing/to be nothing', there is a strained, oddly formal angst at work.

On the other hand, the hard man in *Fivemiletown* steps out from the screwing fairly chastened with good old northern ire in his belly: 'how the fuck', 'shit scared' and 'why give a shit' is, after all, part of what we really are.

There is something far too literary and outraged about Paulin's use of language in this book. This self-consciousness contrasts sharply with, say, the prose writing of Dermot Healy; the need to appear crude, to show ordinary people in the throes of real life, strikes me as an understandable but dated reaction against the Gentility Principle. Who uses terms such as 'lunk July', 'bum hour', 'scroggy town', 'gummy warmth', 'yompy farts', 'dwammy sick' or the cold expression of an 'oral childhood'?

One tires of the quizzically knowing semantics and, eventually, impatience grows into disbelief that this is where we have ended up:

> ... that story with its thoughtful prisoner,
> miles of salt-marsh and a word like *wesh*.

Floating in the background of *Fivemiletown* is a pissed-off, disenchanted figure. The book seems to hover with 'him' between disenchantment and disgust, without ever artistically revealing why. We are to take all this on faith.

While the good poems struggle for a bit of air (poems like 'The Red Handshake', 'André Chénier', 'Peacetime', 'Were the Rosenberg','Voronezh' and 'An Ulster Unionist Walks the Streets'...), the rest thrash around, bearing grand titles like 'Defenester' and 'The Defenestration of Hillsborough' until 'The Caravans of Luneberg Heath' and Heidegger's miserable duplicities summon the end and the following haunting lines:

but what nature is
and what's natural
I can never tell just now

I think it is a shame that Tom Paulin, a poet whom I greatly admire and will continue to do so in spite of the worst that *Fivemiletown* can do to me, is barking up the wrong tree. Inspiration must lie elsewhere.

## V

In that marvellously committed and lopsided book *ABC of Reading*, Ezra Pound blasts: 'The critic who doesn't make a personal statement is merely an unreliable critic. He is not a measurer but a repeater of other men's results'. Much of what goes for criticism at present is either unreliable self-serving puff or heavy-duty world-view-enforcement. Which is to say, we know the opinion beforehand. It's rare for a literary critic to speak his or her mind about how good a book is and why.

Tom Paulin's television appearances on BBC's 'Late Review' were certainly a measure of his critical forthrightness and willingness to call a dud a dud. The vernacular performance of bemused seriousness translates, however, oddly to the page. Some of the essays in *Writing to the Moment: Selected Critical Essays 1980–1996* (1996) are reprinted from Paulin's Bloodaxe collection *Ireland and the English Crisis*. They stand up well, particularly the politico-cultural ones: 'The Making of a Loyalist' (1980) on Conor Cruise O'Brien is remarkably prescient given Dr O'Brien's one-time alignment with the absurdly titled UK Unionists; 'Paisley's Progress' (1982) is the best thing written on the subject; and short pieces on Louis

MacNeice and Derek Mahon are sharp, concise and helpful. The bigger statements seem dated and constrained by polemical self-consciousness and a curious anxiety to prove something: 'A New Look at the Language Question', 'Political Verse' and 'Vernacular Verse' brashly identify the intellectual coordinants of Paulin's extensive reading of poetry. The individual poet's art (never mind personality) fade into a structurally articulated plan of action: Elizabeth Bishop's 'sophisticated quietism – or her radical distaste – challenges the democratic Yankee triumphalism of much American verse'; 'Blues singers' are seen as 'the most authentic American political poets' whose 'work challenges the more comfortable written tradition'. Yes, but ... The frank, clear prose, the eye for political deceit and the culturally dubious makes *Writing to the Moment* a powerful gathering of Paulin's formidable and erudite conceptualising of literature, its place in this moment and what he calls, in the title essay, 'a refusal of the literary': the enabling (and self-dramatising) idea of much of what Paulin writes as both poet and critic.

Ireland features quite a bit ('Where the Aran Islands used to be the focus of cultural authenticity, Belfast would now [1987] seem to be the deep navel of ethnic chutzpah') and England, mostly of the nineteenth and early twentieth centuries.

Surprisingly, judgements of contemporary poets and prose-writers are few and far between. Of Tony Harrison, for instance, a poet and dramatist one would have thought close to Paulin's own artistic and intellectual concerns, not much more than a passing reference. The harping on about dialect, local words, argot of one kind or another, and the rattling around for said challenges to 'the more comfortable written tradition' belies an old-fashioned romance with 'orality', the spoken tradition, the natural voice, which strays very close to Colour Supplementese: "Reading these lines 'You shall have a fishy/in a little dishy/you shall have a fishy/when the boat comes in' we need to hear 'boat' not as bot, but as the Northumbrian bisyllabic bo-uht". Paulin's distaste for what he calls southern

Irish writers' 'saccharine gabbiness' is fair enough but the notion that vernacularism is a sure sign of artistic authenticity and a radically acceptable civic consciousness (in Britain or Ireland) should have been left out to dry some years back.

'A writer who employs a word like "geg" or "gulder" or Kavanagh's lovely "gobshite" [*lovely?*] will create a form of closed, secret communication with readers who come from the same region. These words act as a kind of secret sign and serve to exclude the outside world. They constitute a dialect of endearment within the wider dialect'. For brave hearts read claustrophobia and good old-fashioned nostalgia.

These informed essays know exactly what they are about; Paulin's rational discourse is copy-book stuff. While at no stage does Paulin actually challenge received reputations or provoke reassessments of forgotten or neglected writers, the spirit of *Writing to the Moment* is very much of these times and Tom Paulin one of the wizards of 'Uz'.

[1984–1996]

# 'HOW'S THE POETRY GOING?'

Sometime back at a reception for the announcement of literary awards for young and 'promising' new writers, mostly attended by PR people and the sponsors, a well-known academic and writer came up to me. After exchanging a few brief pleasantries (who is ever really relaxed at such gatherings?) he left on the words, 'And how's the poetry going?' I knew he meant well and it was, after all, only an attempt at concerned familiarity, a little like saying, 'Has the bad leg healed yet?' or 'Did the mother-in-law recover?'. The phrase struck me, though, suggesting something that I would like to explore here, if a little hesitantly: the nature of the Irish literary community. I say hesitantly because I am well aware of the pitfalls that lie ahead. Whether one likes it or not, to turn one's attention to the community, large or small, in which one lives or is, to some extent, identified with publicly, can be a dangerous business. It is all very well to question and probe the role of others, but when did we last see or hear of politicians questioning their own structures and ambitions; or the media in Ireland examining their own nature and objectives; or arts administrators and promoters asking beyond the rhetoric, what their function actually is in Irish society today?

My own experience is limited to particular prejudices, the most adamant of which is a constitutional antipathy to cliques or groups of one kind or another. I have always believed that writers, painters, sculptors, all artists need independence and the more mature the culture they come from, the more that independence is guaranteed through schooling and the media. This is not to say that I think writers should exist in glorious isolation; far from it. The civic world, social space, is there to be enjoyed as best it can by all and sundry, irrespective of their work or lack of it. Political responsibilities or commitments are exercised, rejected or ignored by each individual citizen and this includes the writer, of course, who is no different on this score at least.

What concerns me here is the centripetal force that compels writers in Ireland to share basic ideas, ideals and ambitions (a common understanding) on fundamental politico-cultural levels: the assumption that we all are, really, one big (though maybe not all the time, happy) family.

## I

In recent years it has become a vogue for writers to describe themselves as 'full-time writers', as if, like footballers, there are semi-professionals who only play at weekends and hold on to the day-job as well. As someone who has lived precariously enough, balanced between writing and teaching after a short spell as a librarian, to emerge in his late thirties as a writer, I have realised how some office-bound administrators, like T. S. Eliot and Wallace Stevens, librarians like Philip Larkin, secretaries like Stevie Smith, diplomats like Denis Devlin, mothers like Sylvia Plath and doctors like William Carlos Williams, have all devoted their lives to writing in a manner that defies the comfortingly self-regarding phrase of 'full-time writer'.

I think Nadine Gordimer scotched this idea in 'A Bolter and the Invincible Summer' (1962):

> I'm not flattered by the idea of being presented with a 'profession', honoris causa; every honest writer or painter wants to achieve the impossible and needs no minimum standard laid down by an establishment such as a profession.
>
> *The Essential Gesture* (1988)

Irish writers, surprisingly too the 'young' and the 'promising' as much as the 'well known' and the 'established', have an ambiguous and unresolved tension between themselves and the public world of recognition that exists around them. As Dennis O'Driscoll pointed out with characteristic verve in an 'Irish Roundup' published in *Poetry Review* (1989):

The problem, actually, is not that the Irish Republic can be too difficult a place to establish a reputation as a poet but that it may be too easy ... Those with more tenacity than talent will find magazines to publish them, radio slots to broadcast their 'thoughts for the day', arts centres to host their readings, newspapers to publicise their activities ... As I know to my cost, Irish poets are apt to take grave offence at adverse criticism, however mild and well-meant. As a result many discriminating critics gradually eschew the reviewing of local produce altogether, resulting in a dearth of authoritative and independent reviewing. An indifference towards standards is particularly evident in those sections of the media which are willing to yield air space and column inches to self-proclaimed poets on the basis that if you declare yourself to be a poet, you must be a poet; if you declare it often enough and loudly enough, you must be a 'leading' poet.

This urge ('to declare yourself a poet') is so much more to do with recognition than with the rigours of art. And, as Dennis O'Driscoll candidly reminds us, 'indifference towards standards' refers in effect to those channels, forms of attention, that are readily, indeed eagerly, accepted in Ireland whereby the poet and their putative readers know each other and register that a poem has taken place. It is a code-sign under which, all too often, the poet gives what is expected while the discipline of art, that essential gesture, becomes secondary to the business of being a poet.

## II

It is worthwhile taking a little time out to ponder this business. Historically, we can track the available images in Ireland of what the artist is via the dominant presence of Joyce, since in comparison to Yeats, his influence has been the greater because longer lasting inside the country. As Richard Ellmann points out, with *A Portrait of the Artist as a Young Man* completed, Joyce 'had pretty well exhausted the possibilities of the artist-hero'. Discussing Ibsen with his brother Stanislaus, in 1907, Joyce remarks:

Life is not so simple as Ibsen represents it. Mrs Alving, for instance, is Motherhood and so on ... It's all very fine and large, of course. If it had been written at the time of Moses, we'd now think it wonderful.

But it had no importance at this age of the world. It is a remnant of heroics too.

Then, in conclusion, Ellmann summarises Joyce's accomplishment as an artist very much opposed to heroics:

> He objected to slavishness and ignobility; he thought they were fostered by conventional notions of heroism, which turned men and women into effigies. He wished them to know themselves as they really were, not as they were taught by church and state to consider themselves to be. He gave dignity to the common life that we all share.
>
> *Four Dubliners: Wilde, Yeats, Joyce and Beckett* (1987)

It is this anti-heroic side of Joyce that we seem to have lost sight of in favour of the Poet as Hero; a view sanctioned by Irish political history seen from a nationalist perspective. But one cannot be anything but deeply saddened by the legacy of this myth: the endless stream of Behan 'stories', the one about Paddy Kavanagh, what happened to poor Myles the night ... as these men are reduced to actual illness, alcoholism, irrelevant squabbles, vendettas and premature graves: Behan died at forty, Flann O'Brien at fifty-five and Kavanagh at sixty-three. 'Mighty characters': how often has that phrase been used patronisingly of Irish writers?

Since his death in 1967, things have of course changed, but, as Kavanagh himself well knew, changes can often be mere window dressing. In his *Self-Portrait* (1964) he remarks:

> I realise it would not have been easy for a man of sensibility to survive in the society of my birth, but it could have been done had I been trained in the technique of reserve and restraint. A poet is never one of the people. He is detached, remote, and the life of small-time dances and talk about football would not be for him. He might take part but could not belong.

This is Kavanagh speaking: the poet many see as being quintessentially of the People; applauded and held up as an example of the 'true' bardic Irish tradition. For Kavanagh 'the real problem' is 'the scarcity of a right audience which draws out of a poet what is best in him. The Irish audience that I came into contact with tried to draw out of me everything that was loud, journalistic and untrue'. In perhaps the most damning comment of all, Kavanagh declares: 'What the alleged poetry-lover loved was the Irishness of a thing. Irishness is a form of anti-art. A way of posing as a poet without actually being one'. And in the 'Author's Note' to his *Collected Poems*, Kavanagh says: 'I am always shy of calling myself a poet and I wonder much at those young men and sometimes those old men who boldly declare their poeticality. If you ask them what they are, they say: 'Poet'. (Curious that around the same time, the Italian poet Eugenio Montale should remark: 'It has happened that in the face of the massive production of poems that has invaded our country, and not only ours, I have found the title of 'poet' somewhat intolerable.') It is his resisting of the demands of the 'loud, journalistic and untrue' that makes Kavanagh so important. As the Australian poet Les Murray remarked in *The Peasant Mandarin* (1978):

> ... people who should know better seem to have caved in completely to a journalistic ideal of irresponsible excitement; controversy and ill-will are welcomed as 'lively' and 'controversial' when really they are tragic. They make 'good radio', exciting publicity, but they are a symptom of a deadly sickness in our culture.

We may frown at that phrase 'deadly sickness' but as Murray and Kavanagh know, 'the writer's problems are in some ultimate sense the problems of society'. As Cleanth Brooks has demonstrated in his essay 'The Writer and his Community', for a poet like Yeats 'the plight of the poet ... is a kind of measuring stick for the health of the civilisation – indeed one of the most important measurements, that we have'. So how is it then that, in this most literary of cultures (the Irish), certain clichés about poetry remain entrenched in the schools, universities, newspapers and other media?

### III

During the 1980s, I talked to literally hundreds of students North, south, east and west through the Arts Councils' 'Writers-in-Schools' programmes and was constantly reminded of the caricatures still doing the rounds about what 'being a poet' is like. The poet as a lonely, morose figure; a clown; a drunk; an effete, other-worldly creature; a mystic. Poetry likewise is a chore; something to be 'learnt' for exams and that's it, or else a ballady home-spun philosophising about death or grief, the parish or the past: that great poet from Ballymagash? In other words, poetry is something separated as an art-form from their lives. The truly amazing thing is that these clichés have not changed with time in any substantial way. As an indirect result of them, and their complicated causes and effects, many writers in this country either left (like Samuel Beckett and Brian Coffey) or put up with the situation and, in the process, damaged themselves, like Patrick Kavanagh. It was Beckett who wrote so dismissively to Thomas MacGreevy in 1938 of his 'chronic inability to understand ... a phrase like "The Irish People" or to imagine it ever gave a fart ... for any form of art, whatsoever, whether before the Union or after'. And Patrick Kavanagh, often seen as the 'traditional' Irish poet in contrast to the 'cosmopolitan' Beckett, could be equally contemptuous of Irish culture in his *Self-Portrait*. Indeed, the poems Kavanagh wrote are shadowed by this awareness as he attempted to find an authentic image for himself as a poet, caught between terrible bouts of self-consciousness and justifiable rage. In so doing he tried to subvert some of the clichés. Take his poem 'I had a Future', for example, with its poignant concluding refrain:

> Show me the stretcher-bed I slept on
> In a room on Drumcondra Road
> Let John Betjeman call for me in a car.
>
> It is summer and the eerie beat
> Of madness in Europe trembles the
> Wings of the butterflies along the canal.
>
> O I had a future.

What comes through much of Kavanagh's poetry is his realisation that there was not going to be a 'natural community' for him as a poet. He had instead to create one. But the point is that this challenge is unavoidable for any poet. It is in effect the condition for writing poetry in this day and age. To pretend otherwise, as so often happens in Ireland today, is only to highlight those biases and needs in both the individual poet and the society in which they live and write. Only when poets have separated themselves from the past and its heritage and transcended it can they become truly effective and truly themselves as writers. In Ireland this goes against the grain. We seek to maintain the illusion, at the very least, of being *forever* of the one place and of the one people. This might partially account for the popularity of Irish literature abroad: a consolation for jaded post-modern palates. To cut across this loyalty, transforming it and making possible a change in consciousness, is seen as some kind of betrayal or sell-out. As Nadine Gordimer put it, 'loyalty is an emotion, integrity a conviction adhered to out of moral values'. And there is also Beckett's famous credo: 'The artist who stakes his being comes from no particular place. And he has no brothers'. But Irish literature is meant to conform to already existent cultural-political mores or 'loyalties', rather than challenging these or inspiring others to do so on the basis of artistic convictions. For, behind the myth itself (and the caricature of poetry that follows close behind), there is often a masked disdain for, and patronising of, 'The People', together with an exploitation of – and poetic acquiescence in – their historical condition. Rather than showing possible imaginative ways out of this morass, poets and poetry all too often consort with it.

The bitterness, isolation and nostalgia which permeates a lot of what Patrick Kavanagh wrote derives from these disillusioned feelings – of his being, in a way, an exile, stranded in the uncaring city and finding a kind of compensatory community for himself with other like-minded people. Yet, as Cleanth Brooks has it, to 'become a member of a literary clique or to find oneself the object of a cult of readers and followers is not the same thing as to be part of a community. The clique is too close to one's life and perhaps too complacent of one's faults; the cult is too remote and too much given to unthinking adulation'. Kavanagh seems to have hated this business – and who would blame him? Its self-consciousness and claustrophobia must have drained him, as indeed poems like 'Jungle', 'Literary Adventures', and 'The Defeated' suggest. His poetry can be seen as being about the imagination separated from the common life of the everyday, of his being cut off from what he called 'the habitual, the banal'. In their rightful place, Kavanagh sees the usurping literary world ganging up on the vital imagination and the true world of the innocent spirit. It is a powerful, redemptive vision, profoundly influential in Ireland since Kavanagh's death, but one that was culturally sapped of energy by the very society Kavanagh sought to indict. Instead, it lapped up the irascible Kavanagh's frustrated outbursts and continues so to do.

What Kavanagh gave vent to was his need as a poet to be part of the community in which he lived: to find or rediscover a common cause and experience with it on artistic terms. But, while resisting the sentimental populism of his day, the only option available to him was as the cantankerous rebel: 'a terrible man', the role Irish society had (and has) absolutely no problem in accepting or, indeed, expecting of its poets. However, there is a distinct unease, when poetry is taken, not frivolously, solemnly or with morbid introspection, but seriously, like any other art-form. Nothing more, nothing less.

## IV

In 'Epic', one of his best-known and much anthologised poems, Kavanagh recollects 'the Duffys shouting "Damn Your Soul"' and

> ... old McCabe stripped to the waist, seen
> Step the plot defying the blue cast-steel –
> 'Here is the march along these iron stones' ...

Bertolt Brecht, a slightly older contemporary, was coming to terms with his exile in 'the year of the Munich bother' to which 'Epic' alludes. Which was more important, Kavanagh asks: 'the pitchfork-armed claims' or 'the Munich bother', and he answers: 'I inclined/To lose my faith in Ballyrush and Gortin/Till Homer's ghost came whispering to my mind/He said: I made the *Iliad* from such/A local row. Gods make their own importance'. Brecht curiously inverts this reasoning in a poem of 1939 called 'In Dark Times':

> They won't say: when the walnut tree shook in the wind
> But: when the house-painter crushed the workers.
> They won't say: when the child skimmed a flat stone across the rapids
> But: when the great wars are being paid for.
> They won't say: when the woman came into the room
> But: when the great powers joined forces against the workers.
> However, they won't say: the times were dark
> Rather: why were their poets silent?

Later still, Brecht describes his reasons for writing, and the context in which he was to write 'Bad Time for Poetry', where the house-painter again stands for Hitler:

> In my poetry a rhyme
> Would seem to me almost insolent.
> Inside me contend
> Delight at the apple tree in blossom
> And horror at the house-painter's speeches.
> But only the second
> Drives me to my desk.

It does not matter whether we agree with Brecht here or not, and whether that 'only' is just: the point is that poetry is being questioned, along with its function, and not the place or personality of the poet, as is usually the case in Ireland. A crucial shift has taken place away from the individuality of 'The Poet' (and all the old romantic hang-ups and media hype and puff that go along with that outmoded notion) towards sorting out a place for poetry in practice in the world. I think the same can be said for the Russian poets, like Akhmatova, Mandelstam and Pasternak; the self-mockeries of Robert Lowell or John Berryman, or the anti-heroic poetic of Montale.

In a way both Kavanagh and Brecht fought against the orthodoxies and clichés of their own time; one that was stultifying and the other that was literally deadly. While Kavanagh tried to preserve some sort of artistic authenticity in the face of official chauvinistic 'Irishness' and all the other material odds stacked up against him, Brecht was in the United

States in 1947 confronting the notorious Committee on un-American Activities. In a masterly display, he turned the tables against his bland accusers by equating Hitler's attacks on 'un-German activities' with their 'un-American' witch hunt:

> I wish to say that the great American people would lose much and risk much if they allowed anybody to restrict free competition of ideas in cultural fields, or to interfere with art, which must be free in order to be art.

So what we have is a kind of 'symbolic committee' formed out of inherited cultural prejudices and ignorance; a committee that expresses, in a grotesquely distorted way, society at its most conservative and dogmatic, treating 'The Poet' as an alien. As Brecht knew, the assumptions which gave rise to the Committee are never too far from the surface in any culture that restricts, out of fear, doctrine or expediency, what he called 'the free competition of ideas in cultural fields'. Without that real, or, more often than not, imagined freedom, poets run the risk of being the playthings of their own delusions of power.

[1990]

# THE CRITICAL MASS

Hostility to poetry, whether conscious or unconscious, begins when critics assume that poems and myths are only peculiar ways of making factual statements.

W. B. Stanford, *Enemies of Poetry* (1980)

The 1980s saw a major, if subtle, change happen in the social placing of writing in Ireland. Political patronage, commercial sponsorship and public relations seemed to move hand-in-glove with the promotion of 'the Arts'. There was a steady ideological shift towards popularising the arts in general. Editors, commentators, critics and others in the media were encouraged to appear more popular and populist than the next, more tuned-in to the 'real' issues. As an indirect result, audiences became markets, prizes and awards promotion pitches, art 'an angle' and literary supplements, interviews and profiles literarily little more than gossip columns, seeking controversy, or recycled publishers' blurbs.

Popularity, accessibility and entertainment turned the key words of recognition into a byword for artistic success. What this all meant in creative and imaginative significance was no longer primary. Any hint of critical circumspection was caricatured as academic and elitist posturing. And in a way this kind of aggressive eagerness was useful in so far as it blew away for good the cobwebs of the past which cloyingly gathered around the very (pious) idea of literature in Ireland. Similarly, the tired acquiescence in the impression that writers were two-a-penny and taken very much for granted also went, more or less. The 1980s, ironically, gave a sense of dignity back to writers if only because writing was seen as a money-spinner; a good PR ploy.

Books, paintings, films, music: all were praised or sifted through on the pretext and strength of what they disclosed about the hidden Ireland of sexual repression, political hypocrisies and so on. These were the days of 'self-disclosure' on a national scale – a literary equivalent of The Oprah Winfrey Show. Indeed the American parallel is there for all to see, if we are to go by what Robert Hughes has said:

> In America there's this astonishing lock between therapeutic sanctimony and the profit motive. Art is their church. It was sold to the raw republic as improving experience, in terms of spiritual edification. Nothing whatever to do with sensuous enjoyment or sharpening the old eye. Passionate moralising about the arts began very early on. So if you question this or, worse, say that something is rubbish, it's not an aesthetic disagreement but a moral one.
>
> The Irish Times, 23 May 1992

The state of Irish art has become similarly influenced by a confessional morality. It is, too, the very kitbag that we hear and read about daily in the media. Journalism and art consequently draw ever closer, to such an extent that it can be difficult to tell them apart. Novels, poems and plays once given critical legitimacy in this way can often seem, on cooler reflection, away from the hype, deeply flawed and derivative.

The documentary imperative became dominant as Ireland turned this way and that, obsessively trying to find a new vision of, and for, itself. This insularity created, by turn, a species of superficial cosmopolitanism and, in reaction, a retrenched nativism which has not caught hold so far.

The symbolic moment came (and had to, as many justly believed) with the election as president of Mary Robinson. In that isolated event an imagined alternative took root which overcame the familiar realities of Irish political and cultural life. The possibility presented itself, and still does, that coherently structured imaginative campaigns can change people's lives or, more modestly, influence how we perceive ourselves – which almost amounts to the same thing. Yet such genuine cause for celebration should not eclipse the real and intransigent economic, moral and political problems which the country faces.

In these circumstances, there is a danger that 'the Arts' are used as a kind of smokescreen for the lack of political will in addressing these issues. 'The Arts' are set up as a high-profiled, yet impotent, moral 'opposition'. Writing and writers run the risk of being conned into a game of pass-the-buck – bearing or beating the humanistic heart as institutional power and authority looks on, bemused. But this show will not change much, and change is what is at issue now. It is at the core of all the current agendas – change for the better, based upon a more honest understanding of past failures.

But in the 1980s, the republic of letters became a commercial enterprise, an adjunct of the tourist business, as one pre-eminent arts commentator happily and proudly declared. Writing was looked upon in a materially different way than in previous years. It was a change, not of accent or emphasis, but of direction, ideologically linked to the altered perceptions which conservation-centres and heritage theme-parks enact regarding our relationship with nature, landscape and history. This substantial cultural change was facilitated with little or no questioning and is almost now complete.

For it was much easier to get a poem published in Ireland in the 1980s than it was to find a job. Indeed, there may be some kind of curious link between an economic recession and the number of people who started to write poems or short stories. For those who may well have been quite happy living their lives thinking of 'some day' becoming writers, many have actually made that commitment, possibly on the basis that there was little else to do. Ireland is, we are told, a literary culture, so why not, what is there to lose?

Consequently, poetry is everywhere. Books are published by the new time – first collections are launched, sold on the night, occasionally reviewed, stockpiled, and sometimes poets are interviewed, given prizes, but, more than likely, books are forgotten within the year. This speed of turnover has become mind-boggling for a country the size of Ireland, with its concentration of media in Dublin (or Belfast) producing high-visibility screenings of one writer or another, usually in the form of light entertainment. As one normally unacerbic writer remarked in a fit of pique: 'You can't throw a stone over your shoulder without hitting a poet on the head.'

There is, of course, nothing new about all this flourishing. People wrote poems by the tea-chestful in previous generations and we have Patrick Kavanagh to thank for his comment on the standing army of Irish poets. As a partial consequence, artistic ambition is usually seen in Ireland as pretentious; the common touch a sign of real genius. We are to take our poetry neat, like our politics, undiluted by criticism.

Looked at in the clear light of unexasperated and impartial day, writing poetry is an activity that has consoled and given enjoyment to many hundreds of thousands of people, and long may it do so. There is the risk though that much of this writing is promoted as self-expression similar to the American obsession with poetry as therapy, public and private. Yet letting it all hang out can lead straight to poetic sag.

The problem begins (and ends) when the reception writing receives sidesteps any reasonably detailed literary evaluation in favour of a media coverage which is uninterested in, and often actively hostile to, poetry as an art-form. Maybe there is a constitutional antipathy between both forms of communication? Who knows? Eugenio Montale predicted in 1952 that art was developing in two directions: 'a utilitarian art not unlike sport for the masses' opposed to 'true art as such, not so different from the art of the past and not easily reductible to cliché'. However one is to view the situation, writing became an alternative lifestyle in the Ireland the 1980s. As Robert Hughes remarked of the New York art-world of the 1980s: 'Never had there been so many artists, so much vying for attention, so many collectors, so many inflated claims and so little sense of measure' (*Nothing If Not Critical*, 1991).

Names are in print, photographs taken, discussion (of a sort) follows and out of the anonymity of a personal life, something 'greater' beckons. What that something is, is an illusory sense of freedom; of being a writer. But why should this be so? Why should writing in Ireland carry this extraordinary responsibility to offer up opportunities which are not available in the wider society?

In John McGahern's short story 'High Ground', an exchange takes place between the alcoholic schoolteacher, Master Leddy, and some of his former pupils:

> Ye had the brains. There are people in this part of the country digging ditches who could have been engineers or doctors or judges or philosophers had they been given the opportunity. But the opportunity was lacking. That was all that was lacking.

'The opportunity was lacking': so in a society with closed access to opportunities, the tendency to view writing as a privileged alternative is very strong. Given then the unemployment disaster that was the 1980s, small wonder 'the Arts' became a viable career-possibility and, within that, poetry was seen as a form of expression and consolation sustained and promoted in public relations exercise, written about in terms of a 'social diary', like a night out in *The Tatler*.

The problem is that poetry is not *only* these things, which is precisely where Robert Hughes' 'some sense of measure' comes in. Yet this issue of judgement and discrimination sits very uncomfortably on our shoulders in Ireland. To criticise goes against the grain and is perceived, colloquially, as a negative, niggardly thing.

Patrick Kavanagh knew the difference of course, that artistic mastery and success is never easy and usually elusive. Much of his critical writings (some of the best work we have on Irish poetry from the inside) deals with this issue:

> For a man in Ireland to have the label 'poet' attached to him is little short of a calamity ... He becomes a sort of exhibit, not a man in and of the world. If he happens to be a dilettante without a passionate faith, he will enjoy this position but if he is a genuine poet, it is an indignity and something much worse. Therefore I announce here and now that I am speaking as a journalist. I have resigned from being a poet and I hope my resignation will be accepted.
>
> 'A Goat Tethered Outside the Bailey', *The Bell*, 1953

What Kavanagh meant here by 'genuine' is the big question, but his ironic mocking resignation begs another: of what happens to poetry (never mind poets) when 'popularity' (as distinct from popular culture) becomes the socially and culturally acceptable norm and literary criterion. For popularity is a dodgy business and to rely upon it as a key to artistic value is questionable. I am not for a moment suggesting that literature depends on the anonymous, unread genius sitting alone in his or her mother's house, remote bungalow or council flat. Anything but. What I am trying to identify is the kind of cultural priorities which emerged in Ireland during the 1980s and have become dominant, specifically in relation to the critical reception of poetry, but by implication literature as a whole.

It often looked as if poets were being turned into commercial representatives who had to sell their 'selves' as wares. The critical interventions were based increasingly around polemical agendas with little relation to artistic achievement. This literary politics is, of course, caught up with the imaginary sense of the power that writing has in Irish society. It also involves, prosaically, state and private patronage, access to the media and the struggle to establish 'a reputation'.

Writing on these themes, the poet and critic Les Murray remarked in *The Peasant Mandarin*:

> We must break the grace-and-favour approach to patronage, just as surely as we must break the link, discerned by the public with ruinous effect, between art and privilege. We have reneged on the old problem of reconciling equality with excellence, and we must take it up again, or else face a new pattern of oppressions and class gulfs.

Reconciling equality with excellence sounds an honourable objective for any poet, and anything which gets in the way of achieving it should be brushed aside. For example, this very notion of 'popularity'. So perhaps the 1980s in Ireland conceal deep-seated problems as much as show the real gains, such as the emergence of several woman poets of impressive stature such as Eavan Boland, Eiléan Ní Chuilleanáin, Medbh McGuckian, Nuala Ní Domhnaill and Paula Meehan. This break-through is the single most significant feature of the last decade.

Alongside this artistic achievement one should also place the phenomenal success of Paul Durcan and Brendan Kennelly in, not only reaching, but creating a new audience for their poetry. This engagement with an audience on emotional and social terms, earthed in common, if unstated, moral and cultural assumptions, has a lot to do with the Ireland which emerged in the 1980s and tells us about that society, in turn.

It was an Ireland pitched into self-searching, shrugging off the coil of the church, sceptical of its politicians, losing confidence in its democracy, and desperately in need of finding out the truth about itself.

Poets like Kennelly and Durcan, along with Boland and others, provided an answer, or a sounding board. And in the soundings they gave, they presented a prolific and ready reckoning which involves both the dark and lighter sides of the Republic's moral nature. Their poems privatise and secularise the confessional demands of the public state of mind, interrogate the traditional, historical roles and see what is going on behind the closed doors of this home, or that institution. It was a society discovering itself, very much in transition.

To invoke critical standards or make artistic judgements in such a context is problematic, to say the least. Any hint of an engaged practical criticism – of doubting the consensus – suggests heretical elitist leanings and privilege in the face of populism's cultural revolt. This ascendancy means effectively the controlling middle-class of modern Ireland, listening out for itself or entertaining manageable images of its own place and a desired history of feeling, instead of ideas.

It is important, therefore, that we nail all this cant about accessibility and so forth on the door of the last decade since, more often than not, what was at stake was a masked form of American-style self-promotion and careerism – Robert Hughes' 'astonishing lock' of sanctimony and the profit motive. It has precious little to do with art. Hand-in-hand with the high visibility of poets in the 1980s, there was also this curious indifference towards the value of what 'got' written: the poem on the page, in other words, with *its* language, structure, shape, as well as the world it assumes to embody and the voice that it articulates. Paralleling this indifference, the 1980s also saw, as we all know now, the extraordinary decay in our public life, and the draining away, via emigration as much as anything else, of the energy and vitality so necessary for the maintenance of a critically alert civic society. Both features define the poetic contours of our cultural life and vice-versa.

Speaking of precisely this present, there is something significant in the relative isolation of a figure such as Thomas Kinsella – an implied indictment which he, in uncompromising terms, laid down in an interview in *The Irish Times*:

> Suspicious of the 'trivialising' current trends of appeasing the popular taste with 'accessibility' [Kinsella] criticises the poet as entertainer. 'Poetry should be concerned with communication, not entertainment ... It's not one of the lucky times. There's a lot of bad poetry, bad poets, bad artists and bad readers.'

There is indeed, but this is also a lucky time, because things are changing. Whom and what mediates these changes is important, be that in artistic or cultural (or indeed, political) terms. For instance, we must not make the mistake of falling for the politically correct statement and acceptable sentiment – regarding the North, for instance, or relations with Britain; or what Robert Hughes rightly calls 'the cant of cultural empire and nostalgia for the lost imperial centre'. In the busyness of such puritanical agendas, loaded with the prescriptiveness of sectional quotas, the poem loses out. And it is this vulnerability which makes poetry so incisive, unpredictable and subversive. As Kavanagh knew, poetry destabilises every impatient effort to turn it into something else. Otherwise a self-deluding and self-promoting chauvinism of the kind which he fought so hard against will descend upon us again.

Poetry does not fit into neat categories of decades, any more than actual life. And this idea of Poetry does not really stand up either. There are only ever books of poems making up a world or a voice or an attitude of mind – a critical presence. Writers and artists believe passionately in the value of what they do. It is that imaginative ambition which needs protection to flourish in a culture convinced of its own ability to make the necessary discriminations from the ground up. This confidence is aesthetic and civic. It is also powerful. It is an ability and practice centrally linked to the educational and political priorities of any country and the way access to these learning and democratic institutions is maintained and broadened. Yet the 1980s made many unhappy with the quality of our democracy and, as an indirect result, too much was looked for in the literature – and too little. For as García Márquez has said, the most revolutionary thing for a writer to do is to write well. Committing the poem to a page, making that right, as well as experiencing the decency of mature critical consideration and the non-deferential respect of working artists, is, in this context, a political act, as Kavanagh put it, of being 'in and of the world'. What I am saying here is little more than that Ireland is now in the same situation as other English-speaking cultures in which the values of entertainment and advertising media have taken over (or overtaken) the complex values of art. Maybe there are no longer publicly acceptable artistic values, anyway, and that the marketing men and women who sell 'units' once called 'books' have won out. In which case, there can be no distinction between the poem (play, film, sculpture, dance, song) and an advertisement, between the genuine and the dilettante. That this post-modern heaven has arrived on the wings of post-industrial capitalism is truly and efficiently apocalyptic.

[1993]

# THE BADLY-LOVED

When Adrian Rice asked me during the summer of 1993 if I would contribute some opening remarks about the theme of a conference he was organising on contemporary poetry, *The Badly-Loved*, I hadn't the faintest clue what I should say. Throughout the summer I kept thinking over this idea of contemporary poetry and feeling somewhat remote from the notion of it as a 'subject'. The summer turned into the autumn and before I knew it, it was only a month away. I telephoned Adrian from Belfast and asked him what did he want me to say: 'Just whatever you fancy yourself'!

Then, as we all know, the North, and Belfast in particular, took an appalling lunge into Jacobean darkness with the string of assassinations, the Shankill Road bombing and further killings.

I felt as if I was back in the Belfast of the 1970s, the deserted fearful streets, the sense of home as a fortress or prison; the city really in a dreadful state. And as with that time, the same issues re-emerged: 'How can a poet write in, and about, such a situation?' During the early 1970s I was trying to work my way through these problems in Belfast, and not making a very good job at so doing. I left and moved to the west coast of Ireland where I settled in 1974 and lived until comparatively recently.

So the first thing I have to say is that it is impossible for me to think, or write, objectively about the relationship between poetry and today because of my experiences in Belfast during the early 1970s.

Yet here we are again, peering over the abyss, watching language literally collapse in the face of these awful events.

One has only to listen to the way politicians use language, to understand George Orwell's comment: 'In our time, political speech and writing are largely the defence of the indefensible' ('Politics and the English Language'). What strikes me so much this time around is the amnesia surrounding such language, as if we all haven't been here before, confronting violence, the immobility of political leadership and the lack of civic imagination inside Northern Ireland. So in talking about contemporary poetry, I have to register the abiding influence that my own Belfast background asserts regarding the twin forces of poetry and the present. I have no choice because it would be dishonest of me to pretend that I could talk about these issues in the *abstract*.

Those of us who were born and bred in northern Irish society realise that the 'Troubles' never could be an exotic backdrop to writing poetry since it was complicated enough living in such a divided society. Consequently, the poetry written out of the North, or in Belfast, can be seen as anti-political for this reason alone. Politics had failed.

I have also felt that too much emphasis has been placed on this notion of 'northern' poetry as embodying a monolithic subject-matter when in fact defiance of one kind or another is everywhere in the poetry.

Ironically, contemporary poetry elsewhere has become much more politicised through issues of how, for instance, gender and race inspire cultural identity and political aspiration. If the situation in Northern Ireland was seen for quite some time during the 1970s and 1980s as leading the critical way, it has now become post-colonially old hat. The agenda has moved on to consider, for example, the second-generation Irish in England and the culturally significant reversal that has taken place now that 'Irish is In'. A far cry, thank God, from the bewildering days in the late 1960s in Earl's Court when we kept our voices down.

The poetry that came out of the political and religious conflict in Northern Ireland is now being viewed with much more circumspection. It is politically incorrect or inappropriately anti-political, which certainly accounts for the hostility, or critical distortion, such poetry has met with from some forms of cultural nationalism and post-colonial critics.

Europe, however, has passed us out in this grim sense, and moved far beyond the ethos of civilian-bombing and the sectarian parcelling up of streets and districts in the appalling attrition of 'ethnic-cleansing' in Bosnia. The rise of neo-fascism and racism, so reminiscent of the 1930s, should also have put paid to the indulgent notion that 'The Irish' are historically blighted to suffer forever as victims. Similarly, an accurate parallel with post-war European experience should finally free us from the idea that contemporary poets in Ireland, or from here, are some kind of *inner exiles.*

Across the water, the phenomenon of Thatcherism led to the concentration of the British state into Westminster, leaving the civic, educational and cultural institutions to look out for themselves. What rose up in response was an intellectual anxiety about the value of art and its ability to salvage some counterweight of authority and influence. This 'crisis' is really a question about how language can be used to create literature when the cultural coordinants of the established political and moral code have all but collapsed. No small wonder that critics and readers in Ireland, Britain and the US, particularly the younger generations, respond most positively to the writer who makes some *effort* to redress this widening gulf with work which is, consciously or not, linked to the general crisis. History, if you will, has become privatised.

The individual poet in Australia, the Caribbean, Canada or Britain is expected to slot in to some categorical imperative, be that cultural or political. Only then can he or she feel that what they *do* is truly 'significant'. The poet is also caught up in the Victim Culture of contemporary society, closely identified with the patronising morality and marketing values of the populist culture which dominated the 1980s.

I dislike this pressure very much and believe it is restricting the resourcefulness of poetry while taking the heat off those in authority. It has urged poets to feel duty-bound, or out of self-protection, to identify publicly with specific communities, imagined or real. And to place before such imagined communities, the kind of sentiments or attitudes which they espouse or collectively experience. One of the contemporary problems a poet faces, therefore, is precisely what this notion of 'community' (or minority as marketable niche audience) means in terms of his or her writing poems. With the media and marketing world currently supreme in establishing *artistic* value, one of the standard procedures for highlighting a particular poet's work is to establish the community out of which he or she comes: by region, gender, ethnicity or a mixture of all three. Individuality counts for very little, unless it can be seen as an eccentric lifestyle. Or, even better, that the community itself is bizarre.

Poetry moves ever closer to the commercial and journalistic value-systems of the advertising and 'pop' industry; the poet portrayed as celebrity stakes. Controversy, as with Tony Harrison's *V*, has got to do with Four Letter Words; not the waging of a vicious class war against a working-class community, effectively remaindered by economic change. Similarly, the more the individual poet suffers in public, or by proxy of his or her imagined community, the more appealing the work. This self-conscious display becomes part and parcel of the artistic personae: ultimately, the poems are literally self-serving. How the putative community 'rates' in the shifting sands of fashion is, finally, the heart of the matter, along with the individual poet's preparedness to play the game.

In Ireland, for example, we have various codewords such as 'inner city', 'minority', 'the periphery', 'the marginalised' ('the underprivileged', as a term, naively suggested a privileged society and was accordingly deleted from more recent discourse). These terms translate, but also neutralise, acute social and economic emasculation into consoling fictions with predetermined themes and lexicon: *inclusiveness*, *partnership*, *redevelopment* and so on. The political responsibility for such injustice being tolerated in the first place is lost sight of in the patronising gestures of admiration for this community or that;

glee at the twists and turns of its vernacular speech; and sentimentalised guilt as the angle of vision turns into the credits.

Any suggestion that *The Waste Land* might be as radical an influence as a gable-end mural, or another documentary novel, sends populist nerves and corporate sponsorship into a glazed look. The superannuated intellectual hounds are out for the blood of suspected elitist tendencies. Such inverted snobbery is a real pity. I have to say on a personal basis that I rarely found it in the various readings and workshops I gave during the late 1970s and early 1980s in prisons, schools and community groups. More recently, however, the understandable rhetoric about accessibility and reaching 'The People' has taken a turn for the worse: ideological axes lifted above the head of artistic liberation. The really important issue in all this is the extent to which poetry is seen as a cultural sideshow to *political* inaction.

In works such as *V* and *The Gaze of the Gorgon*, Tony Harrison has written a powerful political poetry which has brought to book the politicians and political institutions of contemporary England. Yet at no time do you feel that the poetry is weakening as a result.

The trouble begins and ends, however, when poets either wilfully, or subconsciously, position their work inside certain predisposed categories; when poets, in other words, service the media and political world, and seek their patronage instead of standing as best they can apart from it. Not hostile, since we are all in the business of communication, but *separate*.

In *The Literature Machine*, a collection of lectures and talks published in English two years after his death in 1985, the Italian novelist Italo Calvino commented upon the situation in Italy during the late 1970s:

> ... on the one hand, a state of deterioration and corruption in institutional framework, and on the other a growing collective maturity and search for ways of governing ourselves.

Calvino goes on to say that the writer 'is given a chance to fill the space left vacant by any intelligible political discussion. But this task turns out to be too easy (it is too easy to make generalisations without having any responsibility in practice), whereas it ought to be the most difficult task a writer could undertake'. Poets, writers, are duped into a false sense of influence because those who actually *possess* economic power and political authority, with precious few exceptions, lack any credible vision or civic belief over and beyond the immediate ever-spinning world of popularity polls and photo opportunities.

Literature becomes, like the other arts, a provocative diversion: a rash of book-awards; a fleeting news item; a request programme; a safe passage for dissent. The poet is seen somewhere between secular priest and executive manager; but not as an *artist*.

As for poetry itself, there is no doubt but that things are looking better than they have done for quite some time. Poetry is physically around much more these days. It is on the DART and the Underground; poems might one day adorn the inter-city routes both North and south of Ireland; TV programmes are made from poetry.

In the Republic of Ireland there has been an explosion of interest in creative writing throughout the 1980s and 1990s. Culture is everywhere discussed as equivalent to social engineering, with writing the irrigation. This development can slump into awful tastelessness and self-importance, with poets proffering themselves in the media as heroic or historical figures while their poems have a fairly mundane existence on the page. The abdication of critical judgement in this regard has led to often embarrassingly inflated images of the poet in contemporary Irish society. In comparison, there is a feeling abroad that England is disintegrating and that along with this slow decay its literature looks increasingly more lacklustre and straining desperately for effect. If the greatest English poet since Auden, the unforgiven Philip Larkin, described in his poems a downfall of sorts, then the sublime rage of Tony Harrison has countered with a vengeance. The state of England having become critical to anyone with an eye in their head, it is fascinating to see what is happening to poetry that comes from what was once called the British Isles.

Comparisons can be odious. Yet, in their declared anxiety to make a cultural statement of intent, Michael Hulse, David Kennedy and David Morley, the editors of *The New Poetry* (1993), have unwisely placed their anthology beside Alfred Alvarez's *New Poetry* (1962, revised 1966), and in so doing point up the unexciting parallel between one and the other. For in their very knowing Introduction, the editors flit through various categories and orthodoxies of contemporary taste without really justifying what is new in all this poetry: 340 pages and 56 poets, worth.

Whereas Alvarez's polemical Introduction, 'The New Poetry or Beyond the Gentility Principle' was eccentric but, still, stirring stuff, summoning Lawrence to his side and berating 'the pieties of the Movement', there is about Mssrs Hulse, Kennedy and Morley the earnestness of the seminar paper:

> In the absence of shared moral and religious ideals, common social or sexual mores or political ideologies, or any philosophy on the conduct of life, plurality has replaced monocentric totemism.

Much of what they say in their Introduction is absolutely correct but half the time one wonders what it has got to do with poetry. Poets are defined in terms of place, cultural accent and minority status but this verges, betimes, on the ludicrous:

> [Selima] Hill can be read for her emotional impressionism and for an exoticism which recalls Flaubert and that English desert eccentric Lady Hester Stanhope. Her radical contribution is to marry this [*what?*] to a sense of the 'I' that seems Lancanian rather than Freudian, and to a contingent narrative sense schooled on Philip Roth, Virginia Woolf and Max Frisch rather than on any 'great tradition'.

What all this means precisely when one turns to Ms Hill's poems leaves a lot to be desired. I suppose this is my main gripe about *The New Poetry*: that there is a huge gap between the editorial imperatives and the poems upon which so much is claimed. A 'new pluralism' and 'believable role for poetry' is all very good and proper, and every man and woman should be for it, but all it takes is a good poet for the language to live. Like W. S. Graham living out his life in Cornwall, for instance. But 'believable role'?

Far too much of *The New Poetry* is given over to poems that say approximately the same thing in untrying and predictable ways. The really good poets, too, are burdened in this way while the not-so-good, of which there are far too many for any one book to carry, merely drag the lot down to a fairly decent level. There is something in this book for everyone, but little, I'm afraid, that will produce the intense unflinching shock wave which shot through the reader of the original *New Poetry*. I am not suggesting, however, that there is no 'new' poetry worth reading in this anthology. Anything but; the 1970s and 1980s have seen some marvellous new work appear which will be read this time next century. The trouble has to do with what the very best poets are being press-ganged into serving up all too often. This unease ties in with the *reaffirmation* (the editors' word) of 'art's significance as public utterance'.

Poetry is naturally in public ownership. Language, after all, can never be privatized. It is part of every citizen's right to speak his or her mind, no matter what civic, economic, educational or cultural obstacles are stuck in front of them. When critics *expect* poetry to be public, we are all in danger of breathing life back into that commissar of socialist realism, sentimental art, and of praising the spokesperson who states the obvious with rallying cries of consolation. Too often the language is insufficient for the task and the reader is left with little more than a poetic appeal.

Poets like Tom Leonard, John Hartley Williams, Grace Nichols and Ciaran Carson rise above the fray; Nuala Ní Domhnaill too is a marvellous poet. There are some very poor selections, however, from Eavan Boland, Paul Durcan, Matthew Sweeney and Harry Clifton, Irish poets who unquestionably justify inclusion. But where are Julie O'Callaghan, John Hughes, Gerard Fanning and Michael Gorman? Listing who is in or out is a boring old cod of a game but some inclusions struck this reader, at least, as strange, out-of-date or simply daft. The absence of Maura Dooley and Andrew Greig is patently wrong.

So what do we have then in *The New Poetry*? Hopefully an opportunity for the non-poetry book-buying public to have a look at what is being written to a large part in its name. For those who know who they like, the book may well prove a bit of a disappointment, the overall tone much of a muchness. At £7.95 the miraculous Bloodaxe have done it again and offered a *Songs of the Seventies & Eighties*, giving those of us who didn't know of, for instance, Maggie Hannan, the chance to read a real find.

Overlooking the rhetoric of this anthology being 'groundbreaking', brave new poetry, lively and accessible, provocative and challenging, risk-taking in address, broad-based and international in outlook (which just about covers all the exits) Ms. Hannan's 'The Vanishing Point' did the business. Too long to quote in full, too full to quote in bits, her work is reason enough to think that there really is a new poetry for which a much more exacting edition of this anthology could have acted as a go-between. What has got in the way is the cultural flak of our time.

With politics in a critical state, as it unquestionably is in various parts of Europe, the arts are understandably looked to for some kind of answer. The more uncertain and deepseated the crisis, the more likely it is for poets to register this breakdown as best they can, in whatever form they can. The big question will always remain however – just how sufficient our language is for this task, and all the other business which writing poetry entails.

[1993]

# POST-COLONIAL CONFUSIONS

For all the talk, Irish literature, unlike American literature or French, cannot be found in classic and universally acknowledged editions. We have no Independence Day; we have no National Canon. Similarly only a handful of brave, innovative studies carry the entire social history of Irish writing of the past two centuries, from pre-Famine to post-Emergency. It is a shock to the critical system to realise the stark reality of just how scattered and fugitive the historical record presently stands in regard to the lives of nineteenth-century writers and the cultural and economic condition of their lives.

What innate anxiety has kept the lives of Ferguson, Davis, Mangan, Carleton, the Banim brothers, Maria Edgeworth (and on and on and on) obscure? Yet they lived in extraordinary times and the story of their ordinary lives would make for fascinating reading. It might also put into perspective the obsessed preoccupations with 'today's Ireland', and its often conceited, self-regarding modernity.

Ellen Shannon-Mangan's monumental biography of Mangan, published with maximum care and finish by the Irish Academic Press, forms part of a massive undertaking, under the general editorship of the late Augustine Martin and including a panel of scholars, to bring back into print Mangan's entire work – poems and prose. Shannon-Mangan's book is detailed, methodical, erudite and complete. It is an essential read and handles the diversity of material – archival, literary and economic – with skill. The portrait of the impoverished, haunted Mangan which emerges from this biography is convincing, if somewhat inert and encased by the rigours of establishing all the facts governing the poet's short life: a vagabond existence, emasculated by alcohol and drug abuse, and an imagination as haunted and exhilarated as that of Poe or, if much less confident, as Robert Louis Stevenson.

Mangan's afterlife radiates, most famously, in the work of W.B.Yeats ('Nor may I less be counted one/With Davis, Mangan, Ferguson', that 'one' echoing with Mangan's own poem 'The Nameless One') and James A. Joyce ('Mangan has been a stranger in his country, a rare and unsympathetic figure in the streets, where he is seen going forward alone like one who does penance for some ancient sin').

It may indeed be the ironic truth that Mangan handed down an image of the Poet – victimised, ostracised, 'his own worse enemy' – which has characterised popular conceptions in Ireland, and concerning Irish poets, from the late nineteenth century until recent times. As John Montague described it in *In the Irish Grain* (1974):

> [W]hat we find in the work of Mangan [amongst others] is a racial sensibility striving to be reborn; is it strange that it comes through with a mournful sound, like a medium's wail? The true condition of Irish poetry in the nineteenth century is not silence, as Thomas Kinsella has argued, but mutilation. Loss is Mangan's only theme.

The poetic impersonations which Mangan worked at call to mind the early poems of Ezra Pound. The mask of speaking in another's voice, in an extenuated accent, via a landscape of sheer otherness ('In Siberia's wastes/The Ice-wind's breath/Woundeth like the toothed seal') has also common bearings in popular song. The strain which Yeats and Joyce saw in Mangan's life and work was his desire to turn this dramatic posture into great literature.

Alcoholism, a profoundly troubled childhood, poverty, militate without mercy against the vulnerable of any age; given the cultural coordinates of Dublin in the 1820s–1840s, it would have taken a masterful artist of Blakean intensity to convey the apocalyptic social and cultural metamorphoses which were transforming (and transfixing) Irish society from its very foundations.

William Carleton's heart broken 'Author's Note' to *The Black Prophet* (1846) is unforgettably lodged at the heart of nineteenth-century Ireland and subsequent attempts to address its reality:

> – do not the workings of death and desolation among us in the present time give them a fearful corroboration, and prove how far the strongest imagery of fiction is frequently transcended by the terrible realities of Truth?

If Mangan's real counterpart is as an Irish Thomas Lovell Beddoes, the gothic lamentation of his poetry sounds both bizarre and terrifying in its enigmatic evasions and theatrical staging. Given the life of his time and the nature of that life, it is hardly surprising that pathos, sentimentality and, ultimately, self-annihilation should characterise his work.

Ellen Shannon-Mangan has unearthed all the necessary details of that life. What she has left unsaid is the extent to which Mangan was destroyed by a perversely contradictory and colonised provincial society on the brink of disaster, of which Joyce remarked:

> Mangan, it must be remembered, wrote with no native literary tradition to guide him, and for a public which cared for matters of the day, and for poetry only so far as it might illustrate these.

This impressive biography has made a significant first critical step in examining the inner historical life of Irish culture and the provocative truths embodied in such figures as James Clarence Mangan:

> After having as an address No.151 Upper Abbey Street, Mangan had moved out, that is, had been evicted, and from December 1848 his trail is lost for a while. It may well have been at this time that he had a room at No.126-7 Upper Abbey Street. An old photograph shows this building to have been a red brick, three-storey edifice with a bow window. Many rooms, little more than closets, were being let in buildings of all sorts during these years, for again, as when Mangan's father was plotting to get rich by remodelling old houses into tenements, masses of poverty-stricken and starving people were pouring into Dublin and looking for cheap accommodation.

This is the real meaning of revisionism: bringing back to light the buried (repressed?) reality of the past and making available to contemporary readers a version and a vision of historical reality. Those 'masses' were of course the shame that darkens, and is then subsumed into, so much Irish writing from the turn of the century. Strangely, it takes this scholarly and academic life of a largely forgotten poet to bring them back to life.

As it has also taken the distinguished Yeats scholar, John Kelly, to resurrect Mangan's anthology of poets and poetry from the Irish-speaking literary province of eighteenth-century Munster. Prefaced by the fragment of an autobiography which Mangan left behind after his death at 46 years of age, John Kelly's wise and informative introduction leaves the reader in no doubt about the ambition, hope and subsequent lament which made up James Clarence Mangan's brief, energetic but ultimately desolated encounter with Gaelic Ireland. Lacking the spirit of a Walter Scott, or the imaginative resources of a Dickens, Mangan's artistic life was engulfed by the immediacy of an historical transition as it was happening in the shocking and irrevocable shift of an entire complex culture from its own traditional language and way of being into a different, alien and more powerful language, prefigured in his self-distortions, sense of apocalypse and what he himself kept referring to as 'my grand moral malady':

> If I perused any books with a feeling of pleasure, they were such as treated of the wonderful and terrible in art, nature and society. Descriptions of battles and histories of revolutions; accounts of earthquakes, inundations and tempests; and narratives of 'moving accidents by flood and field', possessed a charm for me which I could neither resist nor explain.

About half-way through *The Dual Tradition* (1995) Thomas Kinsella remarks about Mangan's nineteenth century: 'But in a bad time for poetry, with the language spoilt and with the criticism of language and of self inadequate, strength of feeling is as shallow an impulse as [Thomas] Moore's impulse to charm or entertain.' When is it a good time for poetry? is the subtextual question which Kinsella asks in this intriguingly blunt essay on poetry and politics in Ireland.

In the shadow of Thomas Kinsella's blanket decisions about what passes for literary history, there is an abiding sense of outrage at the loss of Irish as the vernacular tongue in Ireland. It is the single most important perception, overshadowing the dynamics of Yeats and Joyce, and the contributions of Beckett, MacNeice, Kavanagh and Padraic Fallon, right to the present of Hewitt, Mahon and Heaney: 'The following commentary concentrates on the times of most adjustment and change. It is not a history of Irish literature but a view of the poetry and some of the other literature which the people on those [Galway] plains helped to produce during a particularly brutal and long-suffering past, when one of that people's greatest losses was the loss of its own language.' That relentless past haunts this book.

With the abandonment of Irish by 'virtually an entire population' and the linguistic supremacy of English, Ireland's literary tradition became dual-natured. *Before* The Fall, assimilation was possible (such as the way of the fourteenth-century Norman Earl Fitzgerald, Gearoid Iarla) but, more commonly, *after*, the way was of dominance, with English the language of conquest.

The noble relationship between aristocracy and official poet eroded with time and military defeat. From the late seventeenth century on, as Kinsella charts the relationship between colonials and the dispossessed, there is a parallel sense of poetry being weakened or levelled out: 'the loss of a discriminating audience'.

By the eighteenth century, poetry in Irish had become 'the poetry of a subject people'. It is precisely this unshakable grasp on a distant past, that burns its way into the very quick of *The Dual Tradition*. By the time we hit the nineteenth century, and the emasculated figure of Raifteiri, 'blind Raftery', there is a tragic hue over everything: 'Raftery's poetry is local: there is no concern for national or wider politics, and no suggestion of a world any further than the next parish. It is a world of the defeated, and there are only the defeated there'.

Kinsella's clipped prose indicts how writing in Ireland in English 'was affected by its involvement' in Victorian England, 'with problems of provincialism added to those of complacency'. Tom Moore's songs sound of 'harp, heartbreak and vague patriotism that passes for Irish still in England and the United States'. Are we back on the trail of an essential and authentic 'Irishness'?

Whether praising Mangan or scrutinising Samuel Ferguson, with 'most nineteenth-century Irish poets', Kinsella asserts, 'it is the flaws in their responses that make their poetry not matter in the late twentieth century'. He then turns to the present. And it is with the here and now that the trouble starts because in defining 'the character of a modern Anglo-Irish poetry', Kinsella's categorical impulses can repress rather than liberate.

Louis MacNeice is idiosyncratically defined as coming from 'a colonial family in Northern Ireland, and fully at home in Britain' – which covers a multitude of sons – until one realises that the real sin is colonial survival. 'The post-colonial impulse is the deciding consideration: primary publication in England is regarded as the desirable norm by most Irish writers and by the commentators.'

'The old colonial element' and 'post colonial confusions' are the nerve ends of *The Dual Tradition* and when they are prodded, one is never sure what will happen: 'A renaissance of some kind in Northern Ireland, some interaction of art with the significant violent reality, would not be surprising given the adequate talents concerned and active'.

It is a great pity that Thomas Kinsella should tarnish his important book with the following interpretation of John Hewitt as one who 'knows that it cannot go on as it is but refuses any dealings with the native tribes – sniggering at them, clowns no matter how dangerous. [Hewitt] finds the difficult first step impossible: acceptance of guilt with its obligations'.

What 'it' is, or was, is the big question that has haunted the Irish imagination like a shadow on the lung; or, some would say, an eclipse of the sun. In the reissue of *The 1916 Poets* (1995) all those curious about the historical struggle for Irish freedom will have a chance to consult the sideshow – namely the poetry written by three of the leaders – Padraig Pearse, Joseph Mary Plunkett and Thomas MacDonagh. For here we have them, the poet-patriots introduced by Pearse's one time secretary, Desmond Ryan.

*The 1916 Poets* can now be read as poetry since the historical revisioning of the Rising has settled into two fairly established, if mutually exclusive, ways of seeing the event. On the one hand, piety in formaldehyde; on the other, glick patronising of their courage and idealism. Such is life.

Going through *The 1916 Poets* one cannot help but register the anxious desire and utopianism of these men. Unrealistic, politically flawed and skirting the historical differences within the country, their belief in themselves was quite a remarkable thing. This book pays homage in its own way to what some would call a marvellous self-sacrificing patriotic instinct, and others describe as the fatal gene of blood-lust.

From the platforms of *feisianna* throughout how many years have little children recited the death-obsessed ecstasies of Pearse's poetry, not quite sure what it all meant?

> Lord, thou art hard on mothers:
> We suffer in their coming and their going:
> And tho' I grudge them not, I weary, weary
> Of the long sorrow – And yet I have my joy:
> My sons were faithful, and they fought.

Romantic agonies also ramify through Plunkett's poetry and the creepy gothick backdrop, awash with biblical walk-ons and personifications, is typical of his work:

> Because I know the spark
> Of God has no eclipse,
> Now Death and I embark
> And sail into the dark
> With laughter on our lips.

The real poet of the three is Thomas MacDonagh and his artistic intelligence and understanding of literature is recorded in that disgracefully neglected classic, *Literature in Ireland: Studies Irish & Anglo-Irish* (1916). (Why has the original work on literature by writers such as MacDonagh, Corkery and the intrepid 'John Eglinton' disappeared?) The Whitmanesque posing that went into many of MacDonagh's poems obscured a much more traditionalist talent, with a fine ear for the strength of ballad and the simplicity of song:

> I dreamt last night of you, John-John
>   And thought you called to me;
> And when I woke this morning, John,
>   Yourself I hoped to see;
> But I was all alone, John-John,
>   Though still I heard your call.

The premonitions of death which mark *The 1916 Poets*, like the yearning for solitude and aloneness, are drawn against the ache of duty and the inevitability of sacrifice. Individuality does not count; the impersonation of a collective voice, the folk tradition, becomes either poignantly accepting of fate, as in Plunkett, or operatically turned-on, even while the rhetorical trip-wires are all too visible, as in Pearse's 'The Rebel':

> And now I speak, being full of vision;
> I speak to my people, and I speak in my people's name to
>   the masters of my people.
> I say to my people that they are holy, that they are
>   august, despite their chains.

This might send us squirming in the aisles but it is often the undisclosed text when Ireland's colonial past is summoned by writers on the subject. 'August' popped up after all in the Proclamation but by that stage the destiny of these men had effectively been sealed, as well as the language of rebellion with which the country has lived, for the best part of eighty years.

Indeed in this most transparent of times, when historical significance rises and falls at the switch of a tv channel, and reputations come and go like yo-yos, Marilynn J. Richtarik's *Acting Between the Lines: The Field Day Theatre Company and Irish Cultural Politics 1980–1984* (1994) has marked a definitive critical focus in Irish cultural affairs. Her book can be trusted for balance and detail and, while it might take too much at face-value, the writer is no fool when it comes to manouevering through the Irish mindfields.

Referring to Brian Friel's *Translations*, Field Day's first production, and the contrary interpretations of the play, Richtarik writes:

Perhaps the most consistent element of the English criticism was its praise for the way *Translations* captured the atmosphere of a vanished time. This focus on the literal over the metaphorical elements of the play may have been partly a way of dodging unpleasent political reflections, but it had probably more to do with English ignorance of Irish history and culture.

That particular cultural battle is over – of challenging English reflections on Irish realities. The booty is the substantial commercial and media interest which English publishers, theatres, universities, festivals and cultural programmes have invested in Irish writing. The English 'ignorance' begot an Anglo-Irish intellectual industry, aligned more, let it be said, with ideological sight-seeing than with actual political change. (Irish ignorance of England, Scotland and Wales is another matter altogether).

It is curious to recall, since that first night in Derry's Guildhall in 1980, just how many critics, journalists and reviewers literally fell over themselves to heap praise upon the Field Day enterprise. Yet in the space of a brief five or six years, how cooling the distance became, and by the time of the publication of *The Field Day Anthology of Irish Writing* in 1991, the theatre company was caught in bruising controversy and scorned for being out of touch.

*Acting Between the Lines* describes a world that has virtually slipped into history, its subtitle, Irish cultural politics 1980–1984 seeming much further away than a mere ten years ago. Why?

The achievement of Field Day, in urging people to think and respond to questions about language, cultural identity, power, national imagery and so on, became the wallpaper of Irish cultural debate. As Richtarik writes in her conclusion: 'What should by the logic of almost all concerned have been a mapping of potential common ground would too often in the next five years look more like a struggle for possession of it'.

Writers are of course on their own. What they need is a rigorous and independent literary criticism, of which Ireland is largely devoid. What should stand out now is Field Day's drama and its theatrical worth – Deirdre Donnelly's marvellous performance in *Boesman and Lena*, Thomas Kilroy's *Double Cross*, Stewart Parker's finest play, *Pentecost*, and Friel's Brechtian *Making History*. And it was the latter which Field Day set out to do – to make history. By the late 1980s there were many who felt estranged by this process or, at best, indifferent.

The real change had taken place in the south. For some time southern writers had struggled to make artistic sense of the northern situation and failed. They turned away from the North, or skirted its bloody reminders of murky old History lumbering along, and tuned into the contemporary experience of their own communities, the familial past and the notion took hold that Ireland could get by without the likes of Field Day. In fact, that Field Day and the whole northern 'thing' was standing in the way of a generation of young, ambitious and thoroughly switched-on writers, women and men, who wanted to move into the floodlights of the Robinsonian republic.

A new word entered the lexicon: diaspora. We were into Europe and the US, not the stodgy old Anglo-Irish stew. Fintan O'Toole caught the mood in his review of *The Field Day Anthology*:

> If you look at the contemporary Irish Drama Section you get the impression of a theatre inhabited only by gnarled farmers, people caught up in the Northern Troubles, and people acting out in one way or another the conflict between Britishness and Irishness.

So from Friel, Seamus Deane, Davy Hammond, Tom Paulin, Seamus Heaney and Stephen Rea to Colm Toíbín, Emma Donoghue, Patrick McCabe, Roddy Doyle, Anne Enright, John Waters, Dermot Bolger, Sebastian Barry, Ferdia MacAnna, Martin Macdonagh a generation-shift merges with a geopolitical one. What possible national ground they all inhabit as Irish writers is (was?) the heady stuff of cultural-political debate. I truly wonder, though, if such issues really matter anymore in the brave new Ireland that is always just around the corner.

[1995–1997]